testify

CHRISTIAN CHAPMAN

Testify
Christian Chapman
ISBN No. 978-0-9819403-1-1

Published by KBM Media, a division of Kingdom Building Ministries,
14485 E. Evans Ave., Aurora, Colorado 80014.

Visit us online at www.kbm.org.
For more about Christian Chapman, visit www.christianchapman.com.

Contents

Acknowledgments

THERE ARE SO MANY PEOPLE TO THANK who helped pray and financially get this project off and running. But first, let me keep it real. I want to thank my Heavenly Father; there is no life and breath without my relationship with Him and His Son Jesus. My life, these stories, they are all driven by my passion to serve the one and only true God, who supplies me with all the grace and love a reckless man of faith like me could ever desire or hope to have. I love you my God and my King.

I would also like to thank my beautiful wife, Amy, who has put up with my outside-the-box ministry, which has included late nights of witnessing at the bar, being a broke evangelist waiting for God's next provision for our family, and messing up many date nights because I witnessed to the waiter who needed Jesus. You are the love of my life, the very soul mate that God knew I had to have. I will always love you and appreciate the awesome woman of God you are. Also to my three stud Old Testament prophets Malachi, Isaiah, and Jeremiah—I pray this book will always be a reminder to you that the church is much bigger than the four walls of a building. Always love people and have an intense desire to make a difference in the lives of those who are hurting and lost. It truly is the very heart of Jesus. I love you very much boys and look forward to the great men of God you will one day become.

To my Mom and Dad, who have been through a lot with me, especially in my rebellious teenage years. Surely you must have been terrified when some of my close friends died because of the lifestyles they chose to live, the very same lifestyle I was living. But you always loved me and sheltered me from the storm as much as you possibly could, and you disciplined me when you knew hitting the bottom was what I needed most. Your guidance, love, and support will never be forgotten and I am enjoying our better days with Jesus. I love you both very much.

Also to the godliest woman I have ever known, my grandmother. You are the prayer warrior that kept me safe and the Proverbs 31 woman that every grandson should hope and desire to grow up around. It was because of you and you alone that I knew who to cry out to that night on the highway when I met Jesus. It was your faith, your prayers, and your teaching in my life that gave me the strength and wisdom to cry out to a Holy God when there was no one else to turn to. I have missed you since your passing, but look forward to seeing you again. Surely you are the most beautiful of all the angels.

Many thanks to all the financial supporters in my life as well as all the people who pray for me daily. To Steele Creek Church of Charlotte, you are the very body of Christ every evangelist should have behind his ministry. Simply stated, without you in my life, the ministry God has called me to would never have happened. He has used your body in many ways to keep me on the street doing what I do best—I love you and thank you.

Also to First Wesleyan of Bessemer City, I would like to extend a thank you for all your prayers and financial support that have helped this resource hit the shelves.

Thanks to all who receive my support letter and pray for me and financially support my ministry. I can't thank you enough, especially in these economic times, that you stay faithful and use your resources to see the gospel go out. I hope this book becomes your trophy as you read what God is doing in my life on the road.

To Kingdom Building Ministries: What would I do without my family? A guy like me doesn't connect very deep for very long, so the greatest compliment I could give you is to let you know that I want to be a part of this great team of God forever! I hope you can put up with me. To Loren Hayes, your sacrifice has not gone unnoticed, bro. I love you and thank you for keeping me on the road speaking and sharing my faith. Also to Adrian Despres and Foster Christy, you are great men of God and I thank you for all your support, love, and guidance.

Also to my great brother in the Lord Tony Halverson and his beautiful family in Charleston: I will never be able to express in words how your prayer, financial support, and phone conversations have helped me continue the good fight. You are the best example I know of a man who serves behind the scenes and gives selflessly so the gospel can be extended. You ask for no fame or glory, a pat on the back or payback. You simply love and give, so I want to acknowledge you in this book and thank you for keeping me and my family safe by giving your life and resources to me. I love ya, big guy!

To Creston Mapes, my ghostwriter in Atlanta: You're awesome, bro, and this project would be empty without your insight and passion for the gospel. I pray that we get to do many more books together that inspire people to be radical followers of Jesus. I love you, my friend, and thank you for your work on this project.

Finally, last but not least, to all the readers of this book. Without purchasing this book and supporting this project the word just wouldn't get out. I thank you for your desire to read these pages and grow deeper in your street evangelism. Remember, discipleship is important, but who is the church going to disciple if we don't evangelize and bring them? I love you and look forward to hearing how God uses this book to radically challenge you to testify. Let me hear from you on my website at www.christianchapman.com.

Peace,
Christian Chapman

Introduction

Then they called them in again and commanded them not to speak or teach at all in the name of Jesus. But Peter and John replied, "Judge for yourselves whether it is right in God's sight to obey you rather than God. For we cannot help speaking about what we have seen and heard."

(Acts 4:18–20)

I JUST LOVE PETER. Sometimes, you'll hear pastors and theologians give him a hard time for nearly drowning due to a lack of faith when he attempted to walk on water to Jesus. Or they'll criticize him for not being in tune with God's sovereign plan when he ripped out his sword and sliced off the ear of one of those who had come to arrest Jesus in the Garden of Gethsemane.

But to me, Peter was the ultimate picture of courage. Throughout his life, both while he walked with Jesus and after his Savior's death and resurrection, Peter was so brimming with zeal and excitement about what Christ had done in his life that he *could not help but testify* about what he had seen and heard.

In other words, Peter's life had been so radically transformed that he literally could not contain himself—he could not keep quiet—about Christ's intervention in his life.

What about us? Is that our experience? Has Christ indeed transformed us?

If so, do we have a difficult time containing all of the extraordinary stories about what Jesus has done and is doing in our lives? Or have we lost our zeal? Have we forsaken our first love?

That's what Jesus pointed out to the Church of Ephesus: "Yet I hold this against you: You have forsaken your first love. Remember the height from which you have fallen! Repent and do the things you did at first" (Revelation 2:4, 5a).

Look, I'm forty years old. I understand we Christians can get burned out. That's one of the reasons I've decided to write this book. I want to help you (and help myself) return to our first love, to remember the height from which we may have fallen, and to repent and do the things we did at first—like sharing with the world what Jesus Christ has done for us and what He died on the cross to do for them.

One day I was listening to a dear friend speak to a large crowd at a church, and right in the middle of his talk, I was quickened by the Holy Spirit and challenged to write the book you now hold in your hands.

Why?

Because this man, this dear friend of mine, was telling everyone else's story but not his own. Now, in no way am I knocking this man of whom I speak. On the contrary. I have heard him speak and have been moved by his words on a number of occasions. Because he served in the military, he loves war stories. He is a true historian, and his tales date from Jesus to Napoleon Bonaparte, from George Washington to today's contemporaries. He is a wonderful communicator and a master storyteller.

I have no doubt this gentleman spends anywhere from forty to sixty hours a week in his office doing research. I'm sure he is a master of Internet search engines. I'm certain he pours over commentaries, quote books, history texts, *The Washington Post,* and *The New York Times* to pull together the most intriguing historical facts to weave into his Sunday sermons for the most powerful impact and takeaway for his listeners.

But the last time I heard the man speak, I began replaying all the times I'd ever heard him over the years and, for the life of me, I could not recall one time when he ever told his own story. Or when he talked about his own family. Or when he shared about his relationship with his wife. Or when he did street ministry downtown. Or when he ever shared his faith with a stranger in line at the store or with a waiter at a restaurant.

In all the times I heard him speak, I never heard him share a story from his heart about his own life and testimony.

That's what challenged me to write this book. I started pondering the power of our testimony. I started understanding that when we are unafraid to share how God has intervened in our lives and transformed us, that's when other people's lives will be impacted for eternity.

"They overcame him by the blood of the Lamb and by the word of their testimony; they did not love their lives so much as to shrink from death" (Revelation 12: 11).

Boom.

Are you challenged by that? I sure am!

It's my prayer that this little book will cause us to return to our first love and to recapture that zeal that once burned in our souls and overflowed from our mouths.

Peter's life was on the line. Sanhedrin officials ordered him to shut up about this Jesus he was advocating. But Peter's faith was real as steel. He feared God more than man. "Who should I obey, you fleshly guys whose measly breath is in your nostrils, or the Almighty God who created heaven and earth?"

It makes me think of that scripture:

"I tell you, my friends, do not be afraid of those who kill the body and after that can do no more. But I will show you whom you should fear: Fear him who, after the killing of the body, has power to throw you into hell. Yes, I tell you, fear him" (Luke 12:4, 5).

Instead of sitting in an office talking about somebody else's stories, Peter lived out the Christian life. And because he did so, he always had fresh stories to tell. Many people in the Bible and throughout history have literally lost their lives because they chose to live passionately for God and to stand and testify by going out and living the Christian life instead of telling other people's stories. They lived passionately for Christ and it often cost them their lives—but they always had a story to share because they were out there "gettin' with it."

What about you? Maybe you're on a spiritual high. You're out there "gettin' with it," testifying about all that Jesus is doing in your life, and reaping some amazing fruit. If so, be humble and thankful. And may this book inspire you to continue to fight the good fight and press on until the Master's return.

For others of you, perhaps you're like the friend to whom I referred, always telling someone else's stories but never your own. Or maybe you find yourself telling stories from ten years ago when you first got saved? Worse case scenario, you don't testify at all.

Brother, sister—whoever you are, wherever you are—my heartfelt prayer is that the stories in this book will shake you to the core. No one can explain away these stories that have happened to me. My hope is that they will inspire you, electrify you, and help you know that, when you have the courage to testify, you are literally rocking Satan's world. And you are bringing hope to people you may not have even realized were at the end of their ropes.

As you read, may the same power fall on you that fell on the seventy-two whom Jesus sent out, two-by-two, into the towns He was about to enter: "The seventy-two returned with joy and said, 'Lord, even the demons submit to us in your name.' He replied, 'I saw Satan fall like lightning from heaven'" (Luke 10:17, 18).

Introduction
Questions to Dwell On

1) Read **Acts 4:18-20**. How often do you let outside circumstances keep you from testifying? What are some of those circumstances and what steps can you take to overcome them and testify?

2) Read **Revelation 2:4, 5a**. People can usually tell what you love most in life just by listening to you talk. Could the people you meet throughout your day accuse you of being in love with Jesus?

3) Read **Revelations 12:11**. Lost people will be set free from sin because of Jesus' sacrifice—period! But how will they know unless someone shares that great story? According to this verse, what is the main obstacle we must overcome? (HINT: It's a four letter word that starts with "s," ends with "f," and has a lot to do with "you.")

4) Read **Luke 10:17, 18**. According to this verse, when we share our testimony, we defeat Satan and cause him to fall like lightning. Have you ever experienced that? Are you ready to experience it more?

One of my favorite actors is Russell Crowe. In L.A. Confidential, just before he beats a confession out of a corrupt lawyer, Crowe says "Here's the Juice." It's another way of saying, "This is the deal, and you better get it!" At the conclusion of each chapter, you'll get the juice.

HERE'S THE JUICE:
If you have been saved and set free by Jesus then you have a story to tell. A story that no one can take away because it is something real and supernatural that happened between you and God. That's why Jesus urged people to return to their first love in Revelation 2:4, 5a. He designed your salvation story and the other miracles you've seen Him perform, and there is amazing power in those things! So, go and share and bear good fruit!

1 - The Journey Begins

Jesus answered, "Everyone who drinks this water
will be thirsty again, but whoever drinks
the water I give him will never thirst.
Indeed, the water I give him will become in him
a spring of water welling up to eternal life."
The woman said to him, "Sir, give me this water...
I know that Messiah (called Christ) is coming.
When he comes, he will explain everything to us."
Then Jesus declared, "I who speak to you am he."

Then, leaving her water jar, the woman went back
to the town and said to the people, "Come, see a man
who told me everything I ever did. Could this be the Christ?" They
came out of the town and made
their way toward him...Many of the Samaritans
from that town believed in him because
of the woman's testimony.

(John 4:13-15a, 25, 26, 28-30, 39a)

EVERY TIME I READ THIS ACCOUNT OF JESUS meeting the Samaritan woman at the well I discover new wisdom about unity, unconditional love, and the incomparable power of a testimony that is shouted from the rooftops. Allow me share a bit about my journey with you, and you'll see why I get so pumped up about what went down at the well that day.

If any of ya'll know anything about racing or NASCAR, you know that Kannapolis, North Carolina, is the home of racing great Dale "#3" Earnhardt. It just so happens to be where I grew up, too.

Racing is in my blood, as it is for pretty much everyone from Kannapolis. I'm a chaplain for NASCAR, love the racing community, and even race Legends cars at the annual Summer Shootout at Charlotte Motor Speedway.

Kannapolis is a small, cotton mill town of about 40,000 people. When I was growing up, my dad ran the local Honda business and my mom worked at The Cannon Mills Company, maker of textile products, such as cotton bed sheets, pillowcases, and assorted linens.

I had a lot of friends and a good childhood. My parents were involved at a local church. All of my needs were provided for. But things started to go downhill for me in about the seventh grade when I began hanging out with people two and three years older than me, people who were drinking and smoking. I was young and always ready and willing to test the waters on the other side of the fence. Unfortunately, I went too far, began dating an older girl, and ultimately lost my virginity.

Being a popular kid who excelled in baseball, basketball, and football, I always felt pressure to live life on the edge and to do daring things no one else would do in order to maintain my popularity.

In about the ninth grade, I noticed some serious friction developing between my Mom and Dad. They were having major issues. My heart broke when I learned that my Dad had an affair. Things turned nasty and my life was sent into a tailspin. I was raging inside. I did not understand how this could happen to my family. And I forced myself to believe I simply didn't care anymore about anything.

One night, when I was in eleventh grade, I came home to a quiet, low-lit house. I'll never forget the feelings of hurt and anguish when I found my Mother passed out at the kitchen table, holding a bottle of Crown Royal in one hand and an eviction notice in the other. The letter stated that we needed to be out of the house by midnight that night or we would lose all our furniture and everything in the house. Later, I found out that my Dad had mortgaged the Honda business and put our home on that same mortgage. So, when he lost the Honda business to bankruptcy, we lost our home, too.

As it turned out, my Dad sent my uncle and some other relatives to the house I'd grown up in for sixteen to seventeen years, to help get us moved out by midnight. When I saw them coming, I was so embarrassed, I took off in my car and refused to return to school. Within a few days, my Mom and Dad not only agreed to separate and divorce, but they also decided to send me to the Oakridge Military Academy in Virginia.

It wasn't a good move for me. I become violent, increased my drinking and drug use, and threw anything that was left of my good sense completely out the window. In fact, along with some other cadets, I broke into the Colonel's house one day and stole all his liquor. I had tallied up 115 disciplinary hours of community service in my time at the military academy.

I was turning into a negative, rebellious, obnoxious young man. One day, I woke up and decided I flat-out didn't want to go to school anymore, so I quit. I have to admit the decisions I made in those days were fast and destructive. I found it much more exciting to make a reckless choice that could lead to death than to face life's often difficult truths.

Soon I was living in Myrtle Beach, South Carolina, with a group of the craziest people I had ever encountered. There was alcohol, pills, weed, fighting, womanizing, and partying around the clock. That became my lifestyle every single day. I couldn't hold a job because I was lost in pride, rebellion, and selfishness. I even committed robbery.

It got so bad that I couldn't even pay my small portion of the rent to the guys with whom I was living. They booted me into the streets. I lived homeless for a number of days. It even got to the point where I would wander up to various groups of people who were cooking out and pretended to know someone at the gathering just so I could get my hands on something to eat and drink. Being homeless for a few days may not sound like much, but when you actually get to the point when you don't know where you're going to lay your head that night, it is daunting, to say the least.

Things continued to spiral out of control as my relationship with my Mom and Dad became completely severed. During that season, I served overnight stints in jail for public drunkenness and driving while having a suspended license.

Then came the infamous drug-run.

That's right, I was running a shipment of drugs from Myrtle Beach back to Kannapolis. Being the upright kind of guy I was, I "sampled" some of the drugs I was transporting. Bad move.

Next thing I knew, my heart was slamming against my ribcage and I was freaking out. I literally crawled into an emergency room that night. Doctors there (I still can't remember what town I was in) said I almost had a heart attack from the drugs in my system.

Leaving the hospital the next day, I had nowhere to turn, so I phoned my Dad. Graciously, he allowed me to come to his home.

I had played the role of a modern day prodigal son. I had squandered everything, lived a rebellious life far outside God's will, then wanted to come back "home." I even told my Dad I was willing to work for him, and was willing to do anything to receive his love and forgiveness—anything to be accepted back into the fold.

My Father made it very easy for me. He not only received me into his home, but he got me a job at Charlotte Honda, where he had become the manager. I started doing some racing, assembled bikes for him in the summer, and began trying to live a productive life. But I still couldn't get away from the party scene.

This was the late eighties. I was seventeen years old. It was a Saturday, and I heard about a party, and went to check it out. It was exactly what I had anticipated: a lot of drinking, pot-smoking, and drugs floating around. Distinctly, I remember thinking, 'Man, this is exactly what landed me in trouble.' Something inside just told me to get out of there. It was one of the first times ever that I left a party without getting high.

Jumping on my motorcycle, I headed back home toward Kannapolis. But at about 2 a.m., my motorcycle ran out of gas on I-85 at Harris Boulevard, a well-known intersection in Charlotte. Not long after I began thumbing for a ride, a car pulled over. Right when it stopped, a taxicab light atop of the car lit up.

The driver flipped on the meter, took me to the closest gas station, I got a can of gas, and he drove me back to my motorcycle. I put gas in the bike, had a brief conversation with the driver, thanked him, paid him, tipped him, and he took off. Then I threw my leg over my motorcycle, ready to roll out, and realized I had left my keys in the taxicab.

That was it.

The life was sucked out of me.

It was 3 a.m. and I'd had it.

As a slow motion replay of my messed-up life began to roll in my mind, I started to cry. The drugs, the crimes, the alcohol, it all came flooding back. I thought of the $1.29 bottles of rotgut wine I used drink, the womanizer I'd become, the bad relationships that consumed my life and my time in and out of jail.

My life had no productive future.

I was sobbing.

I slid off the bike and dropped to my knees, crying loudly, shoulders heaving.

I ripped the helmet off and wept uncontrollably. I could barely get my breath.

Never had I attempted to communicate with God in a meaningful way. I had little knowledge of the Bible but knew God had supposedly done some significant miracles in the past. I'd said some small prayers growing up, but this time would be different. It was all or nothing.

"God!" I cried out, "if you can part the Red Sea, I mean, if you love people enough to split an ocean then surely, if you want to be a part of my life, you can send me a ride."

I buried my head in my hands there on the ground and meant every word I cried, taking my business to the so-called Master of the universe. "Here's the deal, God. I really don't trust You. I really don't know You. I really can't hear You. I can't see You. I really don't even know if I believe in You, but I know that I *need* You. And if You're real, if You really want to be a part of my life, here I am. I mean, I am at the end of my rope, Father."

I got quiet, tried to steady my breathing. My nose was practically in the black cinders. "If You will just send me a ride...I need a miracle in a fresh way. I've never had a miracle, I've never seen one or experienced one, but if You will give me a miracle, I will give my life over to You. I will go to church tomorrow. I will give my life to You. I will never turn back, if You just send me a car—*any car!*"

But I wanted it to be real. I had to see Him move. I had to know for sure. So, I said. "I'm not gonna thumb for a ride because if you're not a God that can make a car pull over, I really don't know if I want You as a part of my life. So, here it is, God, send me a car and I'll give my life to You. But if You don't, I really am going to contemplate going home and ending my life because that's pretty much where I am. I don't even want to live anymore."

Silence.

My face was wet. I opened my eyes and stood.

A car was sitting there. I determined it had pulled over while I had been praying. I'll never forget that car: a navy blue Pontiac Firebird. And my very first thought was, *What a coincidence*. But I soon realized nobody pulls over in Charlotte at three in the morning to give somebody a ride. Not even back then.

So, there I was, seeing this car sitting there, wondering if I had just experienced the first miracle of my life.

I was hesitant and scared as I walked up to the car.

The window rolled down and the console light flipped on.

The first thing I saw was a huge, black Bible sitting in the passenger seat.

Are you kidding me?

My curiosity soared and my eyes went from the Bible to the driver's seat. There sat an enormous black man, kind of hunched over, very relaxed wearing a weight-lifting belt and sporting one of the biggest afros I'd ever seen. It's amazing the small things you remember. But I recall loving afros back then. I was a huge fan of the R&B group *Earth, Wind, and Fire*, and those guys had some of the most beautiful afros I'd ever seen.

So, I was digging the afro, even though I was sporting a very ugly mullet cut and about three earrings. Based on my past experiences, I was nervous and quickly scanned the backseat for weapons. Instead, the back seat was loaded with cases upon cases of Orange Crush soda. There must have been a dozen cases back there.

So, there we were, two guys with absolutely nothing in common. A humongous black man with an afro and a skinny white punk with an ugly mullet and earrings. We looked at each other and, until I die, I will never forget the words first spoken. "Son," he said, "the Lord Jesus told me to pick you up. I would like to share with you about His love."

I practically fell into the car and began weeping uncontrollably.

Clearly, God had sent my miracle.

I was flabbergasted.

And I was quick to fess up to my end of the bargain, as I surrendered my life to Jesus Christ that night there in the front seat of the Orange Crush-laden Pontiac Firebird with the huge black man, whose name I never did get. To this day, my wife insists he was an angel. I've always told her, "Well, if that was an angel, then we're going to be drinking a lot of Orange Crush in heaven."

From that point on, my life has been radically different than it was. Two weeks later, I met the woman who would become my wife, Amy, on a blind date. She "just so happened" to be a Christian. I went back to school, got my G.E.D., then worked as a salesman for Coca-Cola to help put my wife through nursing college.

Next, I was offered a baseball scholarship at Southern Wesleyan University in Central, South Carolina. I played and took classes for four years and graduated owing only $3,000 in student loans, thanks to scholarships and help from my parents. That in itself was a miracle.

My life had been radically changed, and it all started when I prayed a very simple prayer, something like this: "Father, I'm at the end of my rope. I need Your love. I need Your grace. I need Your forgiveness." He overwhelmed me by answering my prayer on the side of the highway that night.

After getting married and graduating from college, I began preaching and have been doing so ever since. I speak at a variety of events, camps, festivals, and retreats for youth and college-age adults, and even people in their twenties, thirties, and forties. I often share my testimony. When I do, I try to help people understand that God is a God of all colors. He is a God of black people, yellow people, red people, white people. He is a God of all cultures. He is one God for all people.

The black man who heard God's instruction and pulled over to help me that night, resembled Jesus in the story of the Samaritan woman at the start of this chapter. Samaritans were half-Jew and half-Gentile. For that reason, they were despised by full-blooded Jews. In fact, the Jews hated the Samaritans so much, they would cross the Jordan River and travel some five hundred miles around the city, just to avoid going through Samaria.

Jesus, a full-blooded Jew, broke down those barriers by going straight through Samaria because He knew there would be a woman there who needed to receive Living Water. The woman said, "Your people, the Jews, hate me. Why are you here?' And He talked to her about the significance of His love being offered to all people, and about her need for something that would bring her true contentment, satisfaction, and peace.

On a side note, I agree with Jim Cymbala, author of *Fresh Wind, Fresh Fire*, who writes that one of the strongest signs of a healthy church is a church full of people of all colors and cultures. It really disappoints me sometimes when I see churches that are full of all white people or all black people, with no sign of diversity whatsoever. In fact, I was so profoundly touched by the man who stopped to help me that my wife and I have adopted three bi-racial boys: Isaiah, Jeremiah, and Malachi. And, like a domino effect, our adoption has broken down racial barriers throughout my entire family.

Jesus knew the Samaritan woman was eaten up in sin. She had been with five people and the man she was with was not her husband. Why do you think she went to the well during the sixth hour, the hottest part of the day? Because she knew no one else would be there. She was an outcast to her own people and a leper of sorts to the Jews on the other side of the wall.

Can you imagine how she felt?

I can.

In a way, I felt the same that night in Charlotte when my motorcycle ran out of gas and I lost the keys. That was it. Enough. I'd had it.

Yet, Jesus went to the Samaritan woman and offered her Living Water. She received it, and because she received it, she then went and shared it with other people in Samaria. It says in Scripture that many Samaritans believed because of her testimony.

The man who picked me up did the same thing.

This is a challenge to all of us.

Would we do what Jesus did? Would we do what the man in the Firebird did? Pick up a white punk in the middle of the night who is freaking out on his knees at the side of the road, eaten up by his own sin? The man who stopped had nothing in common with me. But it wasn't me he was out to please. It was God. He listened and was obedient to the Holy Spirit.

I gave my life to Christ because of that man.

The Samaritan woman gave her life to God because a man named Jesus cared enough to stop and talk to her and share of God's love.

Never again have I met the man who stopped to help me. But I will meet him again in heaven, I know that.

What about you?

Have you gotten alone with God lately? I urge you to do so. Just get quiet before Him. Be still and know He is God. Ask Him to help you see all of your sins. Confess them. Repent. Remember the radical miracle He worked inside of you. Ask Him to rekindle the fire that once burned in your heart.

As sure as that man—or angel—with the Firebird full of Orange Crush was waiting for me when I lifted my head, Jesus will be there for you. And you won't be able to contain the fire He sets ablaze in your heart!

Chapter 1
Questions to Dwell On

1) Read **John 4:3-39**. Jesus didn't have to go through Samaria while traveling to Galilee. He could have walked around it like the rest of the Jews. How often do you sidestep an opportunity to testify and share your God-story? Pray and consider walking through "Samaria" the next time you're faced with an opportunity to testify.

2) Read **John 4:28**. Notice how the woman left her water jar to go and share her story with other Samaritans. She no longer cared about her physical needs because her spiritual needs had been met. How often do we turn down opportunities to testify because we are concerned only with fleshly desires?

3) Read **John 4:39**. Notice how many Samaritans believed because of the woman's testimony. How many people could you have impacted since your conversion experience if you shared your faith everyday? It's not too late to start now.

HERE'S THE JUICE:
My life was changed forever because one man decided to walk through Samaria. Know this: walking through Samaria won't win you a popularity contest. It won't win you the Homecoming King or Queen award. It won't get you the top-rated job with the office view overlooking the city. It won't make you the life of the party or everyone's best friend. But it will make a difference for the kingdom, and kingdom things are all that last anyway. So, set your compass for Samaria and testify!

2 - Wild Wings

If anyone is ashamed of me and my words in this adulterous and sinful generation, the Son of Man will be ashamed of him when he comes in his Father's glory with the holy angels.

(Mark 8:38)

IS IT JUST ME or have we in the West lost our zeal for spreading the gospel and sharing the miraculous, personal testimonies of how God, through Jesus Christ, has saved our messed up souls?

I am afraid that two very ugly and cancerous characteristics—apathy and fear—have crept into our contemporary "Christian" lifestyles. They threaten to quench the Spirit of God and, therefore, prevent those around us from experiencing abundant life here on earth and eternal life in heaven.

My heart's cry is to inspire you, to get you fired up again about the transformation God has designed in your life. I want us to look at the courage and boldness and passion of Peter and to see that we needn't worry about the obstacles in our way or fear the persecutions planned for us. Instead, we must kneel at the front line of the battle, be courageous, and share the transforming power of our testimonies, whenever we can and wherever we go.

Have you ever seen the movie *Braveheart,* starring Mel Gibson as Sir William Wallace, a Scottish knight known for leading a resistance during the wars for Scottish independence? Wallace was regarded as both a patriot and a national hero. At one point in the film, after a narrow victory, Wallace and his men decide to leave the celebration party, and one of the leading Scottish nobles looks at him and says, "William, where are you going?"

I think that this noble felt that he and the men had been courageous once on the battlefield and that they needed time to rest and lick their wounds. Sir William Wallace, on the other hand, felt his men needed to press on and do whatever needed to be done to receive freedom.

"I'm going to fight the English," Wallace responds.

"William, you cannot do that. Are you mad? You're going to lose."

"Why can I not do that? You are so busy squabbling for the scraps from Longshanks' (Edward I, King of England) table that you've missed your God-given right for something better. You think that the people exist to provide you with possessions, but I think that your possessions exist to provide the people with freedom. And I go to make sure that they have it."

Whoa! I absolutely love that part of the movie. And it gets better, because soon Wallace walks outside and is followed by Robert the Bruce, who eventually becomes one of Scotland's greatest kings. The young, soon-to-be-king says, "I'm right there with you, William, but these people are never going to give up what they have. Their titles and their land mean too much to them."

Wallace faces him. "People do not follow titles; they follow *courage*. If you would just lead them, they will follow you." And then he says something very interesting. He says, "And so will I."

When I last watched *Braveheart*, that portion of the movie hit me like a ton of bricks. It utterly changed me and challenged me at the same time. It made me want to be so much more courageous with my faith. If I would have been wearing a Scottish kilt and sword, I would have been charging with these guys, whacking heads, and probably getting my own head whacked!

The bottom line is this: when we *experience* or *witness* someone living their life courageously, we want to be courageous with them.

There's a true story of a Yankee soldier who betrayed the men with whom he was supposed to be fighting during the Civil War. It happened on several occasions, however, the last time he tried to run from the battlefield, he was caught and sentenced to die by hanging the next day. When Abraham Lincoln found out about the man and his acts of cowardice, he penned a note of pardon and ordered the man to return to his unit to fight with his men.

The man accepted the pardon, fought in the very next battle, and died courageously on the battlefield, fighting for the North. When they opened the man's uniform to examine his wound, they found the note from Abraham Lincoln. As the story is told, the soldier who was once a coward found the ability to be courageous on the battlefield and even give his life for something he believed in. Why? Because someone believed in him. Someone believed in the cause. Someone found him to be someone who could be courageous. Then, he believed in himself.

The various biblical letters and accounts of Peter's life prove him to be a perfect example of courage. When he was in the boat with all the other disciples, Jesus reached out a hand and said, "Come, Peter."

What did Peter do? He walked out onto that water. He did it. He went. He walked on H^2O! And, yes, his faith failed when he realized the danger and became afraid. And, yes, he began to sink, and Jesus had to save him. But my point is, where were the other disciples? Within what other disciple did Jesus see that kind of courage or potential? And who else actually jumped out and walked on water? At least Peter got out of the boat.

Look at Peter later when Jesus asks the disciples, "Who do people say that I am?" It was Peter who answered with the truth: "You are the Christ, the Son of the Living God." Jesus replies, "Peter, you're a rock and on you I'm going to build the foundation of my church."

Right after that, Jesus told them He must go and die in Jerusalem, and Peter boldly says, "No, Lord, you mustn't go. You must stay with us. We must protect you." But Jesus whirls around with his back to Peter and says to the man he had just called a rock, "Get behind me,

Satan!"

Imagine the disappointment and shame Peter must have felt.

Later, Peter draws his sword and attempts to defend Jesus with his life. He cuts the servant Malchias's ear while trying to protect Jesus. Then he says, "Look Jesus, I am going to go and die with you." But he ended up betraying Jesus three times. Although people sometimes focus on that, I say at least Peter said he would go and try. At least he lived a courageous life. Filled with the Spirit in the book of Acts, in his very first sermon to the very people who crucified Jesus, Peter preached and three thousand people gave their lives over to Christ.

Although Peter made a lot of mistakes and sometimes made commitments he couldn't keep, I believe he was one of the most courageous figures in the New Testament. Eventually, he became a walking, talking, loving, preaching example of his Savior, Jesus Christ. Peter was so courageous, in fact, that he ended up being crucified upside down on a cross because he said he was not good enough to be crucified upright, like his Savior.

One memorable night, I had the opportunity to "live out" my faith as Peter did so often. On this particular evening, I received a phone call from my dear friend, Marcus Dilly, from the R&B group Primary Colors.

"Christian, it's Marcus," he said. "Let's go down to Wild Wings."

For a bit of background, Wild Wings Bar & Grill is one of the most happening joints in Charlotte.

"It's late," I said. "I don't know if my wife's gonna let me go out."

"Ask her, bro," Marcus said. "See if she'll let you go."

I told Amy about the invitation and she said, "Okay, but be home by twelve o'clock. You're a married man. You don't need to be out late!"

So, Marcus and I ended up down at Wild Wings for what turned out to be Karaoke Night. The place was slammed wall-to-wall with what must have been about three hundred people. As we entered, a humongous bodyguard checked my I.D., stamped my wrist, gave me a band, and we went and sat down. The music was blaring. People were up there singing country songs, flopping off bar stools, falling off the stage; I mean, it was just full of all kinds of crazy people.

Right away, Marcus felt like doing some singing. He's got an incredible voice; he's a white dude who sings with really deep soul. He sounds just like Brian McKnight. At one point in his career, he had a number one R&B hit, "If I Only Knew." He's appeared on Soul Train, Jenny Jones, and other shows, and has opened up for Will Smith and Nelly.

So Marcus gets up there and sings this beautiful Brian McKnight song, "One Last Cry." I mean, he is belting it out with the incredible voice and all of the women are just falling out. They're calling their friends on their cell phones, holding their phones up to the stage so their friends can listen to him sing. People are dancing, swaying their arms side-to-side. Everyone is going crazy, and when it's over, he gets this huge ovation.

Meanwhile, I'm sitting there doing what I do best; I've got like thirty wings in front of me, and I got my little napkin in my shirt like some kind of loser, right? I got wing sauce on my face and I'm saying, "That's my boy! That's my boy, Marcus!" And he comes back to the table and all these people come over to talk to him, and I'm just glad to be a part of it because I'm feeling pretty important as well. All these people talk to him, they're swapping numbers. "You need to come sing on my album!" "Hey, I've got a song you'd love!" "What's your web site?" Yada, yada, yada.

After things calm down, Marcus joins me with some wings of his own, more people are doing their thing on stage, and Marcus suddenly says, "Man, Christian, you need to get up and do one of your rap songs."

"I'm not doing a rap song in here tonight," I replied

"Come on, man," he says. "You know when you do those youth conferences, you take those Snoop Dogg and Dr. Dre lyrics and you put Christian lyrics over top of 'em. That's what you need to do!"

"Dude, I'm not doing that in here," I said.

"Come on, bro," Marcus urged. "Be courageous for the Lord. Stand up. Let people hear your faith. Come on!"

He kept talking to me and challenging me, so finally I said, "Alright, I'll get up."

I'll never forget the karaoke guy. He was drinking a Bud Lite when I approached him. "What you gonna do Big Country? You gonna bring some Tim McGraw?"

I laughed and shook my head. "You would think that, wouldn't you? But no, what I'm really gonna do is some Snoop Dogg and Dr. Dre."

He was like, "Man, are you sure you wanna do that?"

"Yeah, man," I said, "I'm gonna break it down. I want you to do 'Ain't Nothin' But a G-Thing.' But here it is, don't put the words up on the screen for me. I don't need the words. I'm gonna put Christian words over the top. I'm gonna freestyle about Jesus."

He looked at me and said, "Man, are you *sure*? Are you *sure* you want to do that in here?"

"Yeah, man," I said, not so sure. "But if it all falls apart, see that exit door right behind you? Be ready to follow me out because I'll be going for that if they turn on me."

As I waited for my turn, I called my wife and asked her to go into prayer for me. She was like, "Christian, don't do it! Please, just come home. You don't have to do this."

"No baby," I said. "I can't take it back. I'm on the stage. My name's in the pot. We gonna do it. I'm gonna break it down for Jesus."

She literally went into prayer when we hung up.

Soon it was my turn, and when the crowd laid eyes on this big ole country boy they began yee-hahing and yelling, "Bring it to us, Alabama. Bring it!" Obviously, they assumed I was going to perform a country song.

"What's up. I'm going to be doing some Snoop Dogg and Dr. Dre."

The place went dead silent. People put their drinks down, stopped talking, and I'll never forget the big bouncer at the door. I had introduced myself as a pastor when I came in. Well, he just threw his arms up into the air as if to say, "Dude, what are you *doing*?"

I had the attention of virtually everyone in the entire bar and restaurant. A guy on the front row stood up and screamed, "Snoop Dogg and Dr. Dre is in the house. Bring it, big boy!"

"Yeah, man," I said, as he sat down, "but this is my interpretation of Snoop Dogg and Dr. Dre, high on Jesus."

I will never forget the look on his face, I still laugh about it today. He kind of looked at the booze in his glass and must have thought, "What am I drinking? Have I had too much tonight?"

The beat kicked in hard and loud, and I began rapping in my best Snoop Dogg voice, which I can do pretty good. It goes something like this:

"One, two, and three to da four...
Snoop Doggy Dogg and Dr. Dre is at the door,
ready to make an entrance to step on up,
because what I tell you, makes you want to jump.
Give me the microphone first, so I can burst like a bubble,
countin' them long beats together, now the devil's in trouble.
Ain't nothin' but a C-thing, baby, one pumped up Christian,
I ain't crazy. The Bible is the label that pays me.
I'm unchangeable so please don't try to change me."[1]

I just broke it down right there in Wild Wings. I mean, I figured since I was up there, I may as well give 150 percent, so I just went for it. There I was, stomping back and forth across the runway, jumping off the stage, throwing my hands up in the air.

I did the entire song and by the last verse, everyone in the bar was standing on barstools, on the seats of their booths, leaning against the

[1] To hear the audio version, go www.christianchapman.com and click the audio file for *Ain't Nothin' But a C-Thing*.

stage, working their hands to the left and to the right. All the black people were going crazy. All the white people were in shock.

The lady behind the bar selling dollar shots and drafts was clanging her bell. People were yelling. People were screaming. The bouncer had his arms in the air, like, "That's my boy, up there!" The entire bar and restaurant just came to pieces. It was an incredible experience. And when I got finished, according to the karaoke guy, we got the biggest ovation he'd ever heard.

Marcus was proud as a peacock. "That's my boy!" he hollered. "That's my boy, Christian Chapman!"

Amazingly, when I walked down off the stage, a long line of people formed. They were waiting to talk to me. We chatted and prayed together about God saving their marriages, setting them free from alcoholism, lifting them out of depression. An amazing revival had taken place that night in Wild Wings Bar & Grill. Even the guy on the front row with the beer bottle and shot glass was standing up screaming, "I love Jesus!" That boy was rappin' the gospel!"

By the help of the Holy Spirit, Marcus and I went in there and made an impact for God that night. We weren't there to get drunk and cuss and gossip. We were in there eating wings, drinking tea, praising God, loving people, and sharing our testimony.

Did it take courage?

Absolutely. I felt like I was on the battlefield that night. At the same time, I believe God used me and instilled in me a courage that drew people like a magnet. Was it me? No, it was all Him. But I let Him have free reign in me that night. And here's what I have since realized: those people in Wild Wings were all created by and loved by God.

Have they chosen to walk outside of God's will and love? Yes, they have. Let's take one of my three sons as an example. If one of them grows up and says, "Dad, I don't want to live under your roof or your rules anymore." I'm going to say, "Son, right there's the door. You've got to live my way or you must live on your own."

That boy of mine may leave, but if he does, I still love him. No matter what he does or where he goes, no matter how he decides to live his life, I will always love him. And I really believe that's the way it is with God. Even though some people have chosen to walk outside the grace that God has extended to them through Christ's death and resurrection, he still loves them.

When the people at Wild Wings heard me rapping about Jesus, when they saw me living out my faith courageously, it was as if their souls started jumping, screaming, and shouting for something they longed to have: a relationship with Jesus. I believe some of them didn't even know why they were jumping and yelling and shouting, but the Holy Spirit that was definitely at Wild Wings that night compelled them to cry out: "I want that! I need that! I'm separated from that—bring me back to You!"

I tell people all the time to live out their faith courageously. Testify courageously about this man named Jesus. Fight the good fight, and know that Jesus is going to be with you, and you will have the victory.

Will it be easy? Not always.

Will there be persecution? It's almost guaranteed!

After our success at the Wild Wings in Charlotte, I decided to break it down for Jesus at the Wild Wings in Charleston, where I was visiting some friends for a few days. However, the karaoke man at this venue was not open to the Christian version of Snoop Dogg and Dr. Dre.

In fact, he took the microphone from me. "You can't freestyle about Jesus in here," he said. "It's not allowed. You've got to do the real lyrics to the song."

"I'm not doing the lyrics Snoop Dogg and Dr. Dre do," I said. "I'm a Christian. So I'm not going to rap that way. If I can't rap about Jesus, I'm not going to rap."

"Well then," he said, "I'll have to ask you to get down from the stage."

As I retreated from the stage, people began booing. One man in the crowd arose and started cursing the karaoke man, who had to gently calm the infuriated crowd. They were angry. "I'm sorry," the karaoke man said, "we have rules in here that I cannot break."

Interestingly, people came right up to me saying how sorry they were that I was unable to do my thing. They appreciated the fact that I was trying to share my faith through a contemporary rap song. That instance showed me that, even at times when we feel we have not been victorious, God is moving behind the scenes and accomplishing His will in people's lives.

Peter is a great example of courage for Christ. He stepped out of the boat. He drew his sword. He preached by the power of the Holy Spirit. Were there mistakes in his life? Yes, glaring ones! But a cowardly Christ-follower he was not.

Be courageous with your testimony. There is life-changing power in the story God has written of your life. If you step out of the boat, He will give you the power, words, faith, and wisdom to change the world for Him.

> *How beautiful on the mountains are the feet of those who bring good news, who proclaim peace, who bring good tidings, who proclaim salvation, who say to Zion, "Your God reigns!"*
>
> (Isaiah 52:7)

> *Have I not commanded you? Be strong and courageous. Do not be terrified; do not be discouraged, for the LORD your God will be with you wherever you go.*
>
> (Joshua 1:9)

Chapter 2
Questions to Dwell On

1) Read **Matthew 14:22-29**. What is the most important word in this passage? To me it is the word courage. How have you been courageous for Christ lately? Here is another word that might help, "Come!" This is an invitation and actually a command from Jesus Himself to live a radical life of faith and to step out in stormy places and testify. Why? Because in stormy places, what we accomplish will not be done in the flesh but through the power of the Holy Spirit. Read Joshua 1:9.

2) Read **Isaiah 52:7**. Also find the story in chapter two about the Civil War soldier and read it again. What do this verse and this story have in common? Both have the theme of encouragement, of offering hope to someone. The soldier could never have laid down his life if President Lincoln hadn't believed in him and offered the beautiful story of forgiveness. The lost people in Wild Wings that night received the same message—a message filled with good news, peace, good tidings, and salvation. What do you give people when you testify?

3) Read **Mark 8:38**. We better get this one right! If we are ashamed of the gospel, God will be ashamed of us. Nothing should frighten us more than going to heaven to face judgment and having Jesus say, "You were ashamed to share me, so I am ashamed to know you, depart from me." In what ways do you show you are ashamed of being a Christian? Do you keep quiet about your faith around your friends at school? Around the boss at work who is an atheist and pushes his agenda? Around your professors at school who teach and support evolution instead of creationism? Bottom line: if you let others dictate when you share and how you live out your faith, then you are ashamed of the relationship you have with Jesus Christ.

HERE'S THE JUICE:

At the end of *Braveheart*, the queen who has fallen in love with William Wallace tries to get him to save his life by begging for mercy and saying his fight against the English was wrong. He doesn't do it—not even to save his life. He says this to the young queen: "All men die, but not all men truly live." Paul would say it this way, "To live is Christ, but to die is gain." Testify and live strong for Jesus. Never be ashamed of the gospel or of the grace that set you free. I learned in Wild Wings that I have what the world needs, and so do you! The sad fact is, "All Christians die, but not all Christians truly live." Which will it be for you?

testify

3 - Spirit-Empowered

On the evening of that first day of the week,
when the disciples were together,
with the doors locked for fear of the Jews,
Jesus came and stood among them and said,
"Peace be with you!"
After he said this, he showed them his hands and side.
The disciples were overjoyed when they saw the Lord.
Again Jesus said, "Peace be with you! As the Father has
sent me, I am sending you."
And with that he breathed on them and said,
"Receive the Holy Spirit..."

(John 20:19–22)

HAVE YOU EVER "MANUFACTURED" AN OPPORTUNITY to testify? You know what I mean, kind of "forced" your testimony when God really wasn't in it? I can recall doing so many times and feeling later that I had shared my faith legalistically because that was what I was "supposed" to do as a "devout" Christian.

I'm here to tell you that one of the most vital things we must do to become vessels God can use in a mighty way is to begin each day in prayer. In fact, when it comes to testifying, prayer is essential. Prayer is key.

Why?

We need to make sure that it is the Holy Spirit who opens up each opportunity to testify instead of us trying to manifest an opportunity on our own.

When my feet hit the ground in the morning, I try each day to say,

"God, today is all about you." I slowly recite the Lord's prayer, going through it with meaning, praising His majesty, thanking Him for salvation and all He's done in my life, asking forgiveness for my sins, then making specific requests, and pleading with Him for opportunities in which the Spirit of God will move through me.

A quick note here is that it is vitally important to confess our sins to the Father. That way, we have a clear conscience and we're ready to be used.

> *In a large house there are articles not only of gold and silver, but also of wood and clay; some are for noble purposes and some for ignoble. If a man cleanses himself from the latter, he will be an instrument for noble purposes, made holy, useful to the Master and prepared to do any good work.*
>
> (2 Timothy 2:20, 21)

> *Create in me a clean heart, O God, and renew a steadfast spirit within me. Do not cast me from your presence or take Your Holy Spirit from me. Restore to me the joy of your salvation and grant me a willing spirit, to sustain me. Then I will teach transgressors your ways, and sinners will turn back to you.*
>
> (Psalm 51:10-13)

Notice that King David didn't teach sinners the ways of God until he himself had confessed his sins to God. Like King David, I recognize that, in and of myself, I am a very weak man. But He has also helped me realize that, with Him living inside me, I am a powerful vessel that He can use to move mountains. That's why I pray often throughout each day, asking God to do miracles and to open doors of opportunity for me to testify. When I'm tracking with that, things usually go very well. In fact, life is just downright exciting, and I begin to know what Jesus meant when He said He would give us life and give it to us more abundantly.

Not too long ago, my son Malachi and I got into my wife's Honda Odyssey minivan to go someplace. The Odyssey has the buttons that make the fancy sliding doors open and close automatically. It has a lot of cool bells and whistles that excite this forty year old. Since my wife made me sell my 1990 Z-28 Camaro when we started having children, I had to get excited about something! So, I get turned on by all the slick features in the Odyssey.

Anyway, I'm in the minivan and the door won't shut. It shuts, it unlocks, then it kind of rebounds, opening on its own. It will not stay shut. I'm thinking, *What is goin' on here?*

That's when my son Malachi speaks up. "Daddy," he says, "Mommy says the door's broken and you need to take it to the shop to get it fixed."

"When did the door break, son?"

He looked at me and said, "It's been broken a couple weeks. Mommy can't get the door to shut. You've got to push the button to make it shut, go outside real quick, run around the car, and push the door real hard to make it lock so it stays shut."

"I'm not doing that"

I tried it again. It shut then opened again.

"Daddy," Malachi says, "I'm telling you, that's not going to work. You're doing it all wrong. You have got to go around the car and shut it from the outside."

"Malachi," I said, "You know what we are going to do? We are going to pray, because I believe the Spirit of God can shut this door. Do you believe it? Let's pray together."

Malachi looked at me like I was crazy. But we did pray. And, as soon as we were finished, I pushed the chrome from the door and the door actually shut and locked. My son looked at me with an expression of astonishment. "Man!" he said, "I'm going into the house to tell Mommy she's been doing it all wrong!"

I thanked the Lord for that, especially after my son and I had prayed. What a testimony that was for him to witness the power of

God moving through prayer (even if it was something as simple as a car door shutting). I always want to teach my wife and children by example what it means to pray continually as Jesus taught us, to walk with Him constantly, and to consult with Him on every decision.

Let me encourage you to start your day in prayer. Ask God to tap the Holy Spirit into whatever it is we are doing and whoever it is we will be interacting with each day. Ask Him to give us specific opportunities to testify.

Another thing I want to point out is that, because we are only human, we will make mistakes. Look once again at Peter's life. He walked on water, but then he sank. He answered Jesus' question correctly about who Jesus was, but soon thereafter, Jesus called him Satan because he was walking in the flesh and thinking like the world.

Peter didn't want Jesus to wash his feet, and Jesus had to explain to him the example of servanthood he was setting. Peter assured everyone that he was willing to go and die with Jesus, but then he denied Christ three times. In the garden, Peter drew his sword and cut off Malchias' ear, and Jesus had to miraculously reattach the ear and reprimand Peter because He was determined not to fight those who had come for Him.

Peter had many failures.

But remember what Jesus said to Simon Peter and Andrew when He first told them to follow Him?

> *As Jesus walked beside the Sea of Galilee, he saw Simon and his brother Andrew casting a net into the lake, for they were fisher men. "Come, follow me," Jesus said, "and I will make you fishers of men."*
>
> (Mark 1:16, 17)

Jesus calls us to be fishers of men, to go after people, to testify, and to share what we have seen and heard.

Later, once Jesus had been crucified, resurrected, appeared to the disciples, and ascended to heaven, Peter and all of the disciples were just waiting. That's when Pentecost happened, and the Spirit of God descended on them in tongues of fire. Filled with the Spirit, Peter testified, gave his first sermon, and 3,000 people were saved.

That's the key takeaway point in this chapter: we must be filled with the Spirit of God when we testify, and He is the One who must pave the way for us. When we start off our day in prayer and ask God to allow the Spirit to move in our lives, request that He use us in His way, empowered by the Spirit instead of trying to manifest opportunities, that's when we will bear much good fruit for God's will, His plan, and His kingdom.

Here's a real-life example. I call it the State Trooper story. It happened six or seven years ago, and it was one of the most incredible weeks of my life. My job was that of youth pastor at Northwood Assembly Church, located in Charleston, SC. Each year, our church organized a week-long golf and recreation outing at Hickory Knob State Park near Anderson, South Carolina. We traditionally rented all of the cabins, the tennis courts, the pool, everything. It was always just a wonderful week of rest, relaxation, and fellowship.

As the event approached that year, I found myself locked into an incredibly busy week of commitments, and it didn't look like I was going to make it. For the first time ever, I had been called for jury duty early in the week, then I had speaking engagements set for Wednesday, Thursday, and Friday. My wife had told me she was planning to return to Kannapolis to visit her family over the weekend and, by the way, "You're keeping the boys!"

It was that slam-packed, busy week that I had the "dream" opportunity to play golf and goof off with my buddies—all for free! Although I tried to get out of some of my engagements, it just wasn't happening. So, I went to jury duty on Monday and, of all things, the case for which they were selecting the jury happened to be a murder trial. When they began asking me questions, I simply started quoting Old Testament Scriptures, and did they ever run me out of there in a hurry!

By the way, don't ever try to pull any crimes in Monks Corner, South Carolina. That's where I was called for jury duty. When they asked how many of the seventy-five potential jurors owned firearms, almost every single person stood up and started naming the three, four, and five firearms they owned; everyone, that is, except me and three elderly ladies. That's right, only four of us out of seventy-five did not own firearms. So, once again, don't ever try to pull off any funny business in Monks Corner. There may only be a Bojangles and a gas station, but virtually everyone in this small town is packing heat!

After getting out of jury duty Monday, I received a call Tuesday from someone who wanted to share his testimony Wednesday night, meaning I wouldn't have to speak. Then, the next thing I knew, the chapel service at which I was scheduled to speak Thursday had been cancelled. All of the sudden I started getting excited. I wondered, *Is there any possible way I can still make the trip?* Next, I learned that a P.E. teacher who had gotten saved wanted to share his testimony at the event where I had been scheduled to preach on Friday. Things were looking up!

My only hurdle now—and the biggest miracle of all—would be figuring out how to get out of babysitting duty for the weekend. So, I was like, "Okay, God, if You want me to go play golf and hang out with the boys, You're going to have to clear this up."

Unbelievably, my wife called while I was at work and said, "Look, Christian, if you want to go play golf, I want you to go. Your week got clear all of the sudden, and I've been thinking, if you really want to go, I'll back off my weekend plans and you can go have a good time. You deserve a break."

So, man, I was praising God!

My junior high youth pastor, Alan, and I packed all of our stuff into our cars, and we invited two young guys who we were mentoring at the time to come with us. So, we got everything together and took off on what was supposed to be about a three-hour drive to Hickory Knob State Park. We stopped and ate for about an hour at a Ruby

Tuesday's, we stopped for about twenty minutes for gas, and we got lost for about thirty minutes.

Once we were back on the right track, heading down this old, country road in South Carolina, we topped a big hill and there sat a silver Camaro off the side of the road. Remember, I'm from Kannapolis, where everyone has a heavy foot. And I've had enough speeding tickets in my day to know exactly what that silver Camaro was, even though I couldn't see his siren lights or the badge on the side of the door.

Immediately, I looked down at my speedometer, saw I was speeding, and ripped my foot away from the gas pedal. But Alan, who was driving in front of me, just kept the pedal down and kept on digging. I was like, *Oh man, slow down, Alan!*

All of the sudden the Camaro flips his blue lights on and turns around. He's on my bumper in nothing flat. Then he veers around me. Sure enough, it's a state trooper. He hauls past, and my passenger Larry and I begin dancing in the seats, we start singing and celebrating that he hadn't pulled us over.

Next, I called Alan on his cell phone. "Man, you just got busted," I said. "Look in your rear-view mirror, baby."

"Oh no," he said. "I can't believe this."

"You pull over, Dog," I said. "I'm going to the first tee, I'm going to get my golf clubs out, and I'll be waiting on you. After you get your ticket, you come on out and we gonna play some golf." Larry and I were laughing and having a good time. I hung up the phone and we were getting ready to pass by Alan's car and the state trooper's. We were even going to laugh and wave as we went by.

However, as I got ready to pull around them, the state trooper pulled to the left and blocked my path. There was no getting around him. He stuck this humongous arm out the window and pointed to the side of the road, indicating that I should pull over.

I was thinking, "Oh man! Can he do that? Can he pull over two cars at the same time?" But Larry, my passenger, was nervous as a cat.

"Pull over, pull over!" he yelled. So, we pulled over.

This trooper unfolded out of the car (I don't know if you know what I'm talking about, but he was enormous) like one of the Nephilim from the Old Testament. We're talking six-foot, six-inches, probably around 275 pounds. Stiff-brim hat. Starched uniform. He gets out and I can assure you, he wasn't smiling. He stares at me and, without saying a word, just points, as if to say, "You stay in the car, I'll be with you in a second."

"Man, this guy looks serious," I said to Larry, as the trooper approached Alan's car. I pulled my wallet out and started looking for my license, but quickly remembered, as my stomach somersaulted, that I had lost my license several weeks earlier. "Man, I just remembered, I lost my license."

"I want to call my Momma!" Larry yelled.

"No, no, no, no, no," I said. "Don't call your Mom. Just calm down. Open the dash and get my insurance card." He's throwing stuff out of the dash, screaming, "It's not in here! It's not in here. I can't find it!"

That's when I remembered that about two months earlier my wife had asked me to renew our insurance because it was getting ready to expire. But I had failed to put the proof of insurance back in the car. So, there I was, driving a vehicle with no insurance, and I had no license, and I was caught speeding.

Man, this is not good.

Larry was ready to have a cow. "Christian, I want to call my Momma!"

"No," I said, "just calm down. Let's just see what happens."

Finally, the trooper walks back to our car, leans in and says the obvious words, "License and registration."

I replied, "Well, it's funny you should ask that, officer...I really don't have either one."

"Really!" he said.

I tried to explain to him that I had lost my license and what happened with the insurance, and he said, "Okay. You stay put. I'll be right back," he said. "By the way, do you realize you were doing 88 in a 55?"

"88 in a 55?" I said. "Sir, are you kidding?"

"No, I'm not kidding, son," he said. "And without your license, insurance, or registration, you've racked up about $1,500 in tickets. You stay right here. I'll be right back. I want to check to make sure this car belongs to you. Don't you go anywhere."

He walked off and, at that point, I looked at Larry and said, "You might want to call your Momma. We're in some serious trouble." I'm watching all this go down and thinking, *Okay, God, just use this, please, because I'm in some trouble here. I've done the wrong thing.*

The trooper comes back and says, "This car is registered to a Mr. and Mrs. Christian Chapman."

"That's my wife and me," I said. "I'm really sorry. This guy up here in front of me, I know him..."

"Oh, you know this guy?" he said.

"Yes, sir," I said, "that's my junior high youth pastor."

"Youth pastor?"

"Yes, sir" I said, "I'm a senior youth pastor at—"

"You're kidding me. You're one of those Christians?"

"Yes, sir."

"Okay, so let me get this straight. You're a Christian, and you're out here speeding, 88 in a 55, and you have no license, insurance, or registration. You're just a great example for the church, aren't you, son?"

"Actually, not right now," I said. "And I'm not trying to use my Christianity as a crutch, officer, so I want you to go back to the car and write me a ticket, because I deserve whatever you think you need to do. Whatever I've done wrong out here, I need you to write me the ticket for it. I'm not trying to get out of it. I'm living in sin, and I want you to write me the ticket, please."

"Okay," he said. "Hold on a second. I'm trying to take this all in and get this story right. I just can't believe that you're a Christian, and you're out here breaking the law."

"Well, look, what makes me a Christian is not the fact that I'm perfect," I said, "because, to be honest with you, I speed everyday. But what makes me a Christian is the fact that I have a relationship with Jesus. And I'm gonna ask forgiveness for the sins I commit. So, I'm asking for forgiveness right now. 'Father, would you forgive me for speeding and being a bad example.'"

And I looked at the trooper and said, "I'm asking you for forgiveness, too, because I'm being a bad witness. So, would you please forgive me? I apologize."

At that moment, he just stands up.

All I can see is his chest sticking into the window of the car.

I just thought he was writing out the ticket on the top of the car.

He stayed up there about thirty seconds, and when he leaned back down, tears were streaming down his face. His eyes were red. He looked right at me and said, "Son, do you think Jesus can save my marriage and teach my little girl to fall back in love with me?"

At that moment, tears welled up and spilled over from my eyes, and I realized I was in a Holy Spirit-filled moment.

"I've been on my knees praying God would send someone to me," the trooper said. "I went to a church down the street from my house." It was the church of a very large denomination. He told the pastor that his wife had had an affair and he asked the pastor if he would counsel he and his wife. The pastor looked at him and said, "You're wife is going to burn in hell forever because of her sin. You need to divorce her and leave her. You have every right to do that."

If I could have found out where that pastor was, I literally may have rung his neck. That's the worst advice I'd ever heard because our God is a God of love. Jesus hung out with prostitutes. He witnessed to those who had been caught in adultery. There have been many people who have been entrusted to preach the true grace and message of Jesus who just blow it. I was frustrated beyond measure.

But there I was at that Spirit-filled moment, so I explained to him, "Look, man, you prayed for God to send someone to you...let me tell you about my week." I told him about jury duty, my speaking engagements, the babysitting duty—everything that got cleared. I explained that we had stopped at Ruby Tuesday's for an hour, got gas for twenty minutes, and got lost for thirty minutes.

"And here I am, speeding over your hill," I said. "This is a God-divine appointment. God heard your voice, and He's ready to answer your prayer. I want to pray for you to receive Christ, to forgive your wife, and that your daughter's heart will be turned back toward you." (His wife had turned his daughter against him in a vicious way.)

Get a picture of this: Alan is still sitting in his vehicle with the guy he's been mentoring. They're not getting out of their truck. And here's this big state trooper on the side of the road, kneeling down, while Larry and I pray for him to receive the love and forgiveness and grace of Christ. I'm crying. The state trooper is crying. Larry has been crying.

It was probably the most powerful moment I've ever experienced in my life.

The trooper became a good friend of mine. I walked him through the divorce since his wife refused to reconcile and stay in the relationship. She moved on, and he was able to start over and get plugged into a good church. It's cool, because I was sending him Christian literature and he was sending me state trooper stickers to put on my car to get me out of trouble! We had a great relationship and I still call that man a friend today.

It was a phenomenal opportunity and it was all planned and orchestrated by the Holy Spirit. God decided to use me in my weakness. Keep in mind, it wasn't my perfection He used but my weakness. It was me sitting there on the side of the road being a bad example to two young guys we were mentoring and a state trooper; yet God decided to use me to lead a man to Christ.

No man could manufacture such a moment. I couldn't have written a more imaginative story. The whole opportunity was provided by the Spirit. It reminds me of when Peter was filled with the Spirit at Pentecost. He then went out to testify, and from that moment on, God moved through Peter's life to draw unbelievers into His kingdom.

Many times in the New Testament, when Peter was walking with Jesus, Peter tried to manufacture opportunities. He often tried but failed. However, when he allowed the Holy Spirit to have free reign, that's when Peter bore much good fruit for God.

Therein lies our challenge for this chapter: Pray each morning and throughout the day. Plead with the Spirit to lead, to guide, to direct, to open doors of opportunity, and to give us apt words and deeds at *His* appointed time.

Chapter 3
Questions to Dwell On

1) Read **John 20:19-22**. Why is it important for us to be filled with the Spirit of God when we go to testify to a lost world? Read the story of Philip and the Ethiopian found in Acts 8:25-40. The deciding factor of Philip's success was the Spirit (verses 29 and 39).

2) Read **Acts 2:1-41**. Why did Peter have success preaching his first sermon when he had failed so many times in the past? (Key: verses 3 and 4.)

3) Read **Judges 14** (focus on verses 6 and 19). Not only does the Spirit of the Lord give us guidance and open doors of opportunity to testify, but He also protects us and gives us power to overcome obstacles Satan throws in our way to stop us from sharing our faith. Do you feel you are daily tapping into the power of the Holy Spirit to give you strength and guidance in your Christian walk? If not, why not? Make it a point to pray daily for the power and guidance of the Holy Spirit.

HERE'S THE JUICE:
Philip, Peter, and other great men and women of faith had no idea how God was going to use them each day, but they had faith that the Spirit would open doors of opportunity. Remember, the state trooper wasn't saved because I was obeying the speed limit, living a life of perfection, or quoting some witness track I had memorized. It was *all* the Spirit of the Lord guiding me, giving me power to overcome, and using my testimony to make a man search his empty soul and cry out for Jesus to fill it. Don't do *anything* in the flesh, but make God and His Spirit a daily part of everything you do. I promise, if you will let the Spirit lead you and break strongholds, then you will have much success when you go out and share your God stories.

4 - What Kind of Love is This?

"For God so loved the world
that he gave his one and only Son,
that whoever believes in him shall not perish
but have eternal life."

(John 3:16)

A LOT OF CHURCHES TODAY focus on a lot of things besides the most important thing: love.

Not long ago I was speaking at a youth conference at a church up north. After the conference, the pastor got up and said, "I want all of the young people to come down front, and I want people to receive the gift of speaking in tongues."

The longer the event went on, the odder it struck me. It just didn't line up with Scripture. The gift of tongues is a gift God decides to give in His time and in His way. The Bible clearly tells us that along with the gift of tongues should follow the gift of interpretation. God never intended for people to speak out in a church setting in other tongues with no interpretation or organization. In fact, Paul tells us that if we do that, outsiders in attendance will think we're drunk. In addition, I don't believe we can manufacture such a gift and turn people on to receive the gift of speaking in tongues whenever we want. I believe God gives His gifts according to His will and His purpose.

There wasn't much I could do. I had already spoken and that pastor was the shepherd of that flock. So I just sat there as teenagers flowed up to the front. People were on their faces. Some were weeping. Then the pastor said, "Now, I want people over here to start speaking in tongues." All of the sudden, people started speaking in tongues. "Over here," he said. "You guys are not praying in tongues. I want you to pray in tongues!" And to another group of people, he called out, "Speak in tongues. Go ahead. Speak!"

Suddenly, there was just this uproar.

I was down there praying with some of the teenagers and I could see the looks on their faces. Please, don't get me wrong. I would never speak out against the gifts of the Holy Spirit. I love and believe in all of them. However, what was happening before my eyes didn't seem right. It did not align with the Bible. I could see it on some of the teenagers' faces. They were attempting to speak in tongues because they felt out of place, because perhaps they didn't feel "as spiritual" as some of their peers who were speaking in tongues. I'm not laying judgment on anyone because only God knows the heart.

After that segment of the service was over and things were winding down, the pastor said, "I want people to come up and just share your testimony." One after another, teenagers began to file down to the front and share their stories. One after another, each one said the same thing: "I've now been given the gift of speaking in tongues."

After quite some time, surprisingly, the pastor turned to me, handed me the microphone, and asked me to close things out. I kind of looked at him, as if to say, *Are you sure you want me to do this?*

I took the mic, paused for some time, and finally said, "You know, I absolutely love it when people receive gifts from God, and I believe in speaking in tongues, and I believe in healing, and prophesy—but I also believe in 1 Corinthians 13, which says, "If I speak in the tongues of men and of angels, **but have not love**, I am only a resounding gong or a clanging cymbal. If I have the gift of prophecy and can fathom all mysteries and all knowledge, and if I have a faith that can move mountains, **but have not love**, I am nothing. If I give all I possess to the poor and surrender my body to the flames, **but have not love**, I gain nothing" (1 Corinthians 13:1-3, bold mine).

"I have heard many testimonies tonight that you now speak in tongues," I said to the crowd. "But the one thing that I haven't heard tonight is that you now have the gift to love. The Bible says, "'A new command I give you: **Love one another**. As I have loved you, so you must love one another. By this all men will know that you are my disciples, if you love one another'" (John 13:34, 35, bold mine).

The pastor looked as if he'd seen a ghost.

My point was and is that the Pharisees were banging away, trying to figure out what the most important "religious" thing was, and Jesus made it clear and simple: "You will be known as a disciple of mine when the world sees you loving one another." Both Jesus and Paul pointed out that the number one thing we can do, the greatest gift, is to love the Father with all our heart, soul, mind, and strength—and to love our neighbor as we love ourselves.

Jesus said if we would do those two things, we would be obeying all of the law.

I don't think I've ever heard anyone give a testimony in church where they've said, "You know what? I now have the gift to love someone who is homeless, to love my enemy, or to love a person no one else will love."

When I played baseball in college, I had one rule. Every time I went to the cafeteria, I vowed not to sit with the other athletes or with the religion majors. I didn't go sit with any clique. I looked for someone who was alone and I went and sat with that person. Why? Because people need love.

The other day, after I picked my boys up from school, I decided to take them out to eat at Olive Garden. We got to the top of our exit and there was a man sitting at the side of the road who looked really rough. His sign read, "I'm hungry. Please feed me. God bless you." I rolled down the window and said, "You want something to eat? Get in the car."

He jumped in.

"I'm a Christian," I said, introducing him to the boys. "And I just want to share God's love with you. I want to take you out to eat."

He looked at me and said, "Man, I'm drunk. I've got to be honest with you."

"Man, that's okay," I said.

"I really smell and I'm nasty. I really shouldn't be around your children."

"My kids know about the heart of Christ," I said. "You're gonna be fine. You look beautiful to me, brother. Let's go out and eat."

We drove to the Olive Garden. People were looking at him funny, and he felt so guilty that he suddenly turned to me and said, "Man, I can't handle this. I appreciate the heart and thought. I love you brother. God bless you." He walked away with tears in his eyes.

That was frustrating for me. Why? Because that man felt ashamed. Although someone reached out to him, to be Christ to him, the world made it very difficult for him to accept the love being offered. That's why I believe Christians need to start testifying about love. But let me say this—loving people is the most difficult thing we will ever do. Especially loving someone who doesn't love you, loving someone with whom you don't click, and loving your enemy.

Even in churches today, we often seem to love the people with whom we worship because we are like-minded. But we can't worship at the Baptist church down the street or at the Lutheran church across town because we feel different, divided, separated. Too often, we have failed to learn to love each other properly. The Bible tells us love overcomes a multitude of sins. Love should overcome a multitude of differences.

God must instill in each of us this desire and ability to love as He desires. Let me tell you how that happened to me. When I first moved from Charleston, South Carolina, to Charlotte, North Carolina, I was pursuing the idea of planting a church. As I found out very quickly, you'll go broke in a heartbeat planting a church!

I had no money, my wife Amy was working like crazy as a nurse, we had three boys, a house payment, and we had incurred some debt, which we were trying to pay off. No money was coming in from the church, but all of our money, it seemed, was going out! So, I did what many guys do when no money is coming in—I became a landscaper.

In my business, I cut grass and trimmed hedges, cleaned ditches, pressure-washed houses and driveways, dug ditches, and cleaned gutters. It didn't matter what I did, what mattered was that I made money. To that end, I soon became a jack of all trades.

One day, I received a call that would eventually change my life. It came from a man whom I will never forget in Tega Cay, South Carolina. After I arrived at his house, I got out of my truck, saw that he had seven bushes laying out, and took my shovel over to the bushes. I had on my camouflage pants, work boots, and a cutoff shirt that revealed some of my tattoos.

Before I knew it, the man and his wife had come out of the house, introduced themselves, and immediately wiped anointing oil on my forehead. They began circling around me and praying for me. A bit dumfounded, I thanked them when they were finished. And then the man instructed me to plant the seven bushes.

The entire time I worked, the man sat there in the shade, watching me and sipping his lemonade. He never offered me anything to drink. When I was finished, he paid me and I went on my way. The very next day he called and asked me to come back. When I arrived, he told me to remove the bushes from where I had planted them, and to plant them in a different part of his yard.

This is weird, I thought, as I began questioning this guy's motives (and sanity). "Now, you are going to pay me for moving these, right?" I asked.

"Oh, yeah, yeah, yeah," he said.

The same thing happened. He stood beside me, sipping his cool lemonade (as I began to wonder what was in it), while I worked for two or three hours. Once again, he never offered me anything to drink, but just talked and watched me work. I buried the bushes, he paid me, and I went on my way.

Several days later, the man called again, asking me to return.

When I got there, he asked me to remove the bushes and plant them in another part of his yard.

"I have to ask you, why in the world are we burying these bushes again?"

He looked at me, his head tilted kind of sideways, and he said, "Well, they're not growing."

I said, "Sir, you've only had them for four days. Every time I take them up out of the dirt you throw their roots into shock. There's this amazing thing called nutrients. They're in the soil. When you combine those with water and sun, some remarkable things happen! They grow!"

"Well, the sun's not hitting them, that's the problem. I've been watching. It's not hitting them just right."

So, I looked up, trying to figure out how the sun moves over his yard, and I said, "Okay, look, let's plant them over here. They're going to get plenty of sun, and it looks like about the last part of your yard that I haven't already dug up!"

The same thing happened. I buried the bushes, he talked, I listened, he sipped his drink, never offered me any, paid me, and I went on my way.

One week later, the man calls me and asks me to come back.

I literally began to pray because I was so frustrated with this guy I didn't even want to be around him. I wasn't interested in the things he was talking about. He was kind of a nerdy guy. Not athletic, but mega-super charismatic. We just had very little in common. In the most basic of terms, I didn't like him. So, I prayed, "Lord, I don't want to be around this man. You're going to have to help me."

When I arrived, several construction workers literally came running around from behind the house toward their trucks. "Hey guys, what's up?" I kind of held up my hands to slow them down. "What are you guys doing? Why are you leaving in such a hurry?"

"We've been in the backyard working with these people," one of them said, "and they are crazy."

I said to myself, *Man, I realized that weeks ago. Where have you been?*

Then I said to them, "Well, what's going on?"

"We're not going to get into it," he said. "All I can tell you is, we're Christians, and what's going on back there is *blasphemy*!" And they got in their vehicles and drove off.

Being the curious type, I peeked around back to see what was going on. There, I saw the man and his wife digging little gopher holes all over the backyard and planting Bibles in the dirt.

"What on earth are you guys doing?" I asked.

"We're taking this ground back for the kingdom of God," the man said. "It's evil."

Man, this guy has lost it, I thought. So I said, "Okay, you dig your holes and plant your Bibles. What do you want me to plant today?"

Instead of moving the same seven bushes again, he instructed me to mow the yard and put down some fresh pine straw. When I was finished, he paid me, and I took off.

To provide a little more background, during this whole process, one time the man asked me to plant a rose bush by the front steps for his wife. So, I got my shovel and started toward the spot.

"Oh, you won't need a shovel," he said. "The ground where I want the bush is nice and moist."

Sure enough, I got on my hands and knees, began moving the dirt with my hands, and it was really moist and soft. That's when his wife came out. "Christian, do you want a Dr. Pepper?" *Man, I finally get something to drink around here,* I thought.

"Yes, ma'am! I would love a Dr. Pepper!"

She looked down and said, "Sweetie, why are you digging there?"

"Your husband told me to plant a rose bush here for you."

"Honey," she called to her husband, "you know I dump all of the cat urine in that spot. Why would you have Christian dig there?"

That's when I finally lost it. I stood up and said, "Sir, I am going to have to leave and pray right now because I just feel like killing you."

I got in my vehicle, drove away, and prayed. I called my wife and asked her to pray for me. "I don't want to be around this man anymore!" I told her.

That's when Amy imparted some true wisdom. "Christian," she said, "you've been called by Christ to love those with whom you don't get along. Loving someone who loves you is easy, but loving someone like this man is difficult. But that's the heart of Christ. He loved us when we were sinners." Amy has always been a dynamic accountability partner, and I received that message from her.

I also began hearing from the Lord, continually. *Christian, love this man. Love this man. I have a purpose. Love this man.* So I did. Over the next several months, I built a relationship with this man and woman, even to the point where our whole family went over there for cookouts. Once again, I didn't get along with this guy. I didn't click with him. It was difficult for me to be around him, yet I knew that Christ had a purpose.

One day, that purpose was revealed.

Standing in the woods behind his house, we both had our shirts off and were loading lumber into the back of my truck when he got a blank look on his face.

"Are you okay, man?" I asked.

A weird expression had settled on his face.

"Are you going to be alright?" I put my hands on him and he was ice cold, but I didn't think much about it. When I turned to go back to what I was doing, I said, "Are you sure you want to stay out here? You might want to go in the house and rest up a bit."

"No, I'm staying right here."

Within seconds, he fell down and began having a massive heart attack.

When I later described the incredibly violent and grotesque symptoms and gyrations the man had, my wife, Amy, an ICU heart nurse, told me he was experiencing what's known as The Death Rattle. It's when your brain gets no oxygen. You're basically dead, but your body is still going through the dying process. The sounds he made, the things his body did, were awful and horrifying.

I held him in my arms. I don't know a lot about CPR, but I know you can't start giving it effectively until the heart stops beating. So, I kept holding him, feeling a faint heartbeat. I told him I loved him. I told him I was sorry. And I told him to go be with Jesus.

Then there was no pulse. He was blue and ice cold.

I began CPR, which was probably the most difficult and traumatic thing I've ever done. I had to pump his chest. I was talking to an emergency dispatcher after calling 911. The ambulance was on the way; I could hear it down the road. They actually got lost for about ten minutes. Doing the CPR, I could feel his ribs breaking under the compression of my hands. I had to drain the blood out of the back of his throat to clear the way for him to try to breath. I was giving him CPR. It was just a very surreal and gut-wrenching experience.

After it was all over, the ambulance got there and they threw a sheet over him. "Son," a paramedic told me. "If this had happened at the hospital, you couldn't have saved him. His aorta valve exploded. There was nothing you could do."

I questioned God like crazy. I was angry at God. I just couldn't understand why I had to go through that whole process of befriending this man, then going through the whole ordeal of trying to save him. I almost felt like I had done something wrong to deserve all of that.

But in the hours and days ahead, God was quick and faithful to remind me who His Son Jesus was here on earth, and what He went through to show His love for people. He was beaten and spit upon. His beard was yanked out. He went to His death quietly, like a lamb to the slaughter. The Bible says the Lord laid upon Him the guilt and sin of us all, yet He still had the selfless love to say, "Forgive them, for they know not what they do."

As that became evident to me, I realized that, through my relationship with this unlovable man, God had blessed me with one of the best experiences I'd ever had. Why? Because the Holy Spirit empowered me to grow to love a man whom I literally despised. Normally, I never would have had any kind of relationship with this man. But because Christ had called me and enabled me to love and to testify and to live out the message of His love through my life and actions, I connected with a very strange human being.

I had the privilege of preaching at the man's funeral and even played a song on the piano that I had written. After I sang that song at the service, I remember his mom holding me. And I recall thinking, *Just think, this lady held him when he came into the world, and now she is holding the man who held her son when he was on his way out.* It was a really cool experience.

The man's wife approached me after the funeral and said, "Christian, do you know why my husband kept calling you to come back over and do work for us?"

"No, ma'am," but I was thinking to myself that I sure would like to know and that I would love to know why her husband pulled all those crazy stunts.

"My husband has always had a difficult time connecting with people," she said. "Even at the church we go to. He just never really connected." I could imagine why. He was terribly difficult to be around. But I still had a hard time believing no one at his church reached out to him. I struggled with that.

"He called you because you listened to him and you talked to him," she explained. "You even told him you loved him."

It was that simple.

It was all about love.

I had made a difference in his life not because I was a good person but because I obeyed God's Word simply by loving the unlovable. I didn't do it in my power. No way! But with the Holy Spirit indwelling me, with the knowledge of how Christ suffered for sinners on the cross, I could love the man.

God knew this man was coming to be with Him, and I believe the Lord wanted him to experience the love of Christ before he left this world.

What about the people in your world?

Take a look around.

Don't zero in on the people with whom you get along. It's easy to love those with whom you connect, and there's a time and a place for that sweet fellowship.

Instead, look specifically for those who *need* love. Look for people with whom you don't connect. Even resolve to love someone who hates you.

According to what Jesus told us, that's when people will know we are disciples of Jesus Christ the King—when we learn to love.

> *On hearing this, Jesus said, "It is not the healthy who need a doctor, but the sick. But go and learn what this means: 'I desire mercy, not sacrifice.' For I have not come to call the righteous, but sinners."*
>
> (Matthew 9:12, 13)

Chapter 4
Questions to Dwell On

1) Read **John 3:16**. Simple question: has anyone ever loved you this much? How many people out there can honestly say someone (other than God's Son) has actually laid down his or her life for them? It's only happened for me once and that was some 2,000 years ago by Jesus Christ. That is why I always try to give love *freely*—because I freely received. I also know what kind of person Christian Chapman is, yet Christ still chose to die for me out of love. Read Romans 5:6-8. Knowing this, don't you think it's time we start learning to love?

2) Read **Matthew 9:12-13**. Jesus came to love the entire world and to die, but He definitely had a target audience. Search the Gospels for those whom Jesus reached out to most. Does your witness résumé look like His? I have always told people to build their ministry efforts around hurting people. Why? Those people seldom reject the gospel because they have nothing else to hold on to.

3) Read **John 13:35**. What changes are you going to make to your ministry approach, and who will be your target audience?

HERE'S THE JUICE:

The truth is that we can't spread love to the entire world, but we can love those God brings our way. Remember what we learned in the previous chapter—let the Spirit of the Lord open doors of opportunity, and be prepared to walk through them! Even if on the other side of the door is a homeless man, a drug addict, a drunk at the bar, an outcast at school, or someone we just don't think measures up. Remember how you might look to God on a bad day (or even a good one), yet He still chose to send His one and only Son to die for you. As a matter of fact, Jesus cried out from the cross, "Father, why have you forsaken Me?" At that moment in time, God had to turn His back on Jesus because our sin was too disgusting to look upon. So, make sure you love hard and love often. Your very soul may depend on it.

5 - Let it Go

"What good will it be for a man if he gains the whole world, yet forfeits his soul? Or what can a man give in exchange for his soul?"

(Matthew 16:26)

I'M GOING TO SPEAK WITH YOU FRANKLY about something. I'm going to talk to you about losing some of the extra weight that may be hindering you or holding you back from testifying the way God wants you to.

Do you realize it is His desire that we bear much good fruit for his kingdom? I believe there are a lot of us who have one or two obstacles that keep us from sharing our faith. These obstacles may be obvious to you or they may be deceptively "hidden" from view. They may involve fear of persecution, lack of time, apprehension about rejection or embarrassment, apathy, or even issues that we have allowed into our hearts, issues that we've given a greater place than sharing our faith.

At times, even our spouses and children, our jobs, and our hobbies can take preeminence over God. Certainly, those things are important and good, but I believe Christ has showed us in Scripture that He desires to be the most important thing in our lives.

> *"Anyone who loves his father or mother more than me is not worthy of me; anyone who loves his son or daughter more than me is not worthy of me; and anyone who does not take his cross and follow me is not worthy of me. Whoever finds his life will lose it, and whoever loses his life for my sake will find it."*
>
> (Matthew 10:37-39)

Once we give Christ His rightful place, everything else falls into place, including our relationships, our work, and so on.

Personally, I find that when I am not testifying, it's because I have way too many logs in the fire. At those times, I try to lighten the load by getting rid of all of the things that are getting in the way of me being the vessel God longs to use. In my own life, I've determined to cut way back on things like church softball, golf, and even working out at the gym in order to put things back into perspective and to put God back on the throne of my life, where He belongs.

Why is that? Maybe it's because, as I hit the age of forty, I'm recognizing more than ever the truth and reality of David's words when he wrote, "Man is like a breath; his days are like a fleeting shadow" (Psalm 144:4). Life is short—especially compared with eternity. I want to make the most of this vapor of a life down here on earth. I will have forever with my Father in heaven, and that's when my reward will come. But down here, this life is about testifying so others can go with us to heaven.

What is it that holds us back?

Let me tell you a story. Although I batted clean-up all four years while playing baseball in college, I had absolutely no speed. Zero. Now, I could hit the long ball, but when it came to beating out the infield grounder or stealing bases, that just wasn't my thing. I was a power-hitter all the way. The reason I bring this up is because I remember very clearly the first time I ever tried to stretch a double into a triple. I had smacked a line-shot toward the center fielder. He took four or five steps in, then realized he had misjudged the ball, and it shot like a rope over his head.

I was digging for second, saw him approaching the ball, and made the decision to try for third. When the throw came into the bag, I slid, got tagged out, and was furious. I got up, slammed my helmet down, and stormed back to the dugout.

Later, my coach came up to me and said, "You know what, son? It's difficult for me to put a fire under somebody and make him aggressive enough to go for a triple in that situation. It's difficult to motivate someone to do that. I can't teach that. If someone has that fire, it's good. I can always pull back on the reigns, but I cannot impart that fire to anyone. Now that I know just how slow you are, I'll try to hold you up at second next time, but what I'm telling you is that I appreciate your passion. You went for the triple, and I like that. What we need to work on is your speed."

Even though I had the heart to try for third base, to make the most of that hit, there were things I had to work on to be able to get there. So, I applied plyometrics to my workouts, which is a system of exercises that enhances your sprint speed. As I got faster, I ended up getting a few of those triples.

Many people have the heart to testify, like I had the heart to try for that first triple, but very few people have the desire to work at the opportunity and to make it a priority, like I worked on those plyometrics.

Let me challenge you to go beyond the desire of your heart to testify and to take the steps you need to take to actually begin testifying with conviction. Many things can hold you back. Look at Cain and Abel. Abel was pure and honest, while Cain struggled with selfishness and jealousy. In fact, Cain's "issues" caused some terribly destructive things to happen in their lives.

The Israelites were guaranteed the Promised Land, a land flowing with milk and honey, but because the majority of the spies who went to scout out the land for them came back afraid of the giants therein, they did not conquer what was rightfully theirs. The food within was beautiful and the land was rich, but because of their fear, they lived out in the desert until they died.

Samson's one hang up, the one thing that prevented him from being a mighty man of God, was his lust for females. He could have been a great man. But instead, his life was a sad story. There he was, this enormous man of power, but his hair was chopped off and his eyes were gouged out. He was paraded about by the royal officials so people could laugh and jeer at him. Here's this great man of God with this one thing, this one defect, that kept him from living out his full potential.

Look at the rich young ruler, he clearly was a man who had it all together. He could have been a great man of God. Jesus even told him there was just one obstacle in his life—his love for his possessions—and if he would remove that, he would be perfect. But he refused to do that, and we never heard from him again.

In the book of Revelation, Jesus pointed out problems that each of the seven churches were having, things that separated them from living out their faith to the fullest. We all have hang-ups and obstacles in our lives that at times can hinder us and prevent us from being that fruitful vessel God longs for us to be to reach others.

I had one of those obstacles in my life not long ago, and when I realized it and got rid of it, Christ set me free to testify like never before. Let me set up the story for you.

I serve as a chaplain for the Olympic High School football team in Charlotte. During the four years I've served in that role, I've seen some wonderful things happen spiritually on the team and in the community. But there was an instance concerning one coach in particular who I grew to love, Coach McGarity, that was absolutely life-changing.

Coach McGarity was a Marine who served his country faithfully and who had a passion for the game of football. Now, being a Marine, he had some rough language. He used to lose his temper in a heartbeat and he would cuss and really let some people have it. One time while the team was practicing, I was standing on the sideline waiting to go onto the field afterward to do a Bible study with the team. The coach didn't see me standing there. One of the wide receivers missed his route, and Coach grabbed him by the facemask and yelled, "Son, don't you ever miss that route again, or I'll stick my foot so far up your..."

Then he spotted me, out the corner of his eye.

He shook the kids' helmet and said, "Don't you make me cuss you in front of the preacher man again. Get out there and do your job!" He popped the kid on the back of the helmet, the kid ran off, and the coach looked at me and said, "Did I do good, Reverend?"

"Yes, you did, Coach," I said. "Way to pull back on it."

I grew to have a great relationship with Coach McGarity and really came to love the man. He and some of the players used to come over to our house for cookouts during the football season. They were like family, especially Coach McGarity.

At one time, the Lord put it on my heart to do something special for the man. Not long before that, I had won some money racing cars on a Spike TV show called *Reality Racing: The Rookie Challenge*, so I took some of that money and bought a Super Bowl-autographed football signed by the great NFL coach Tony Dungy.

Now, I hadn't purchased the ball for Coach McGarity. No, no, no, no. You see, I have always *loved* Coach Tony Dungy. Before heading overseas to play baseball with Athletes in Action, I stayed at the home of the chaplain for the Tampa Bay Buccaneers when Tony Dungy was the head coach. This chaplain told me so many awesome stories about Coach Dungy and about how much he loved God. I have always been amazed at his testimony.

After Coach Dungy led the Indianapolis Colts to a Super Bowl victory in 2007, I went to an auction at a church where they were raising money for missions. That's where I saw this autographed football, for which the silent bidding started at about $250. I ended up buying the ball for $400. It had Coach Dungy's name and a scripture he had written. It was my prized-possession. My wife even bought me a glass case for it!

I proudly kept the ball on display in the glass case in my living room. I mean, I would wake up in the morning, have my bowl of Cocoa Pebbles, watch ESPN, and just admire that ball. It made for a great beginning to my day. When people came to visit the house, I would walk them right past the photographs of the wife and kids and march them directly over to the glass case. I would remove the ball, show the signature and scripture, and proudly put it back in the case.

Driving one day to the Bible study I was going to have with the football team, I heard God's voice as clear as I ever had: *Christian, I want you to give your Tony Dungy-signed Super Bowl football to Coach McGarity.*

I almost drove off the road.

Literally, I had a moment there where I readjusted my antennae, and I said, "God, that cannot be You. That's got to be Satan. You would never ask me to give up my pigskin. I love that ball."

Very clearly, I heard from Him again. It was almost like the Spirit of God filled up my car and hit me right in the chest. *I want you to give up your football to Coach McGarity.*

"Why?" I said aloud. "Why God? Can't I tell him what I need to tell him, and get him where You want him to be without giving up my football?"

The answer was no, and I'll be honest, I struggled with it. I did not take him the ball. One practice went by. Then another. I did some serious battling with God. But eventually, my heart was so heavy, I gave in.

"Okay, Lord," I said. "If you want me to give this football, if you want to use it for Your purpose, I am willing to give it up because I know You're going to use it. I just believe it."

I took the football, in its glass case, and began marching out onto the football field. Because I had tears in my eyes, some of the guys looked at me and said, "Christian, are you okay?" Can you believe that? That's how selfish I was, tearing up over this football!

"Christian, are you okay?" Coach McGarity approached. "What do you have the football out here for?"

"Yeah, I'm struggling a little bit today, but I'm gonna make it." I turned and yelled to the players. "Gather in here guys, everybody in." As they gathered around I said, "I got something I want to share with everybody." The whole team gathered. "I'm giving my Tony Dungy-signed Super Bowl football to Coach McGarity."

"Yeah!" Everyone cheered and yelled. "Wahoo!!"

"I can't take your football," Coach McGarity said to me.

The first thought that came into my mind was, "Say that one more time and this thing is back in my car!"

"Coach, the Lord told me to give you this football," I said. "Now, here's the challenge. I believe that the Lord wants you to know that you can love the game of football just like Tony Dungy loves football, but you can also love Him, and He can even take you to great places, even like a Super Bowl championship, with Him in your heart."

Tears rushed up and overflowed from Coach's eyes. He took that football. Later, I told the guys, "Now, you hold him accountable. You watch the change that's gonna happen in his life, because God's gonna do some stuff with him." They cheered and clapped, and we went on with our Bible study.

About a month and a half later, Coach McGarity called and asked me if his teenagers could start coming to the youth group where I was youth pastor, at Christ the King Church. "Yeah, absolutely," I said. His teens started coming, and they really enjoyed the youth group. Soon he was calling me and asking me spiritual questions. Then one day he wanted to take me out to eat so we could talk.

As I chatted with him over lunch, he revealed to me that he had an opportunity to become the head football coach at a fine Christian school in Rock Hill, South Carolina. "Man, Coach," I said, "God has you on a journey! God is going to use you in a great way! Through football, God is going to use you. Are you ready? Hold on tight, baby, because the best is yet to come!" He agreed with that. And God proceeded to do some amazing things in Coach's life, in his wife's life, and in his children's lives.

And what had it cost me? One measly Tony Dungy-signed football!

I just spoke with Coach McGarity the other day. He told me that the football sits in its glass case, on his desk, and that many people who come by ask the story behind it. Because the Holy Spirit led me to testify by giving him that ball, lives are still being touched as Coach McGarity now picks up the torch and testifies about what God has done in his life.

Because God helped me get rid of that one obstacle—that one idol—that really held me back, I was able to testify and impact someone else's life. And it can be the same for you. It's requires a daily breaking of ourselves. Learning to deny ourselves, take up our crosses, and follow Him. If we will get rid of our selfishness and our pride and the things standing between us and God, then He can begin to use us to change people's lives.

Chapter 5
Questions to Dwell On

1) Read **Matthew 16:26**. A lot of people probably feel they have conquered the world before their last breath: people at the top of the music industry, the financial elite, actors in their $20 million dollar Hollywood homes, pro athletes, the beautiful that strut New York's fashion runways, and the giants who sit at the top of the financial industry. According to this verse, these people have received their reward in full. How often do you put worldly things before God and the goal of accomplishing His will? Or how about just that one thing that keeps you from sharing your faith and living a more radical life for Christ?

2) Read **Matthew 10:37-39**. When I first read this passage, it sounded harsh, until I understood what it really meant. I tell people all the time that for me to be a good husband requires me to love God first and foremost. Only then can I reflect true and unconditional love to my wife. The same goes for my children. If I don't put my love relationship with my Father at the front of the line, then how can I love my children the way they should be loved, with patience and meekness? Ask your spouse and children if they would rather be loved with a worldly love or a godly love. What relationship do you put in front of God?

3) Read **Psalms 144:4**. I don't know a lot about shadows, but I do know when I was child I would search for shadows for protection from the elements. The only problem was, the shadows weren't around long. As the sun would move and eventually disappear, so would the shadows—and the protection. That is exactly what this scripture says about our lives. It's vital that we make a difference while we're here. Are you ready to put aside relationships and worldly things to build God's kingdom? I pray your answer is yes.

HERE'S THE JUICE:

If you find yourself putting other things before testifying about God's grace, you're not alone. You just read a story about how I struggled to give up a football that was valuable to me so that the word of God could be spread. We can be very selfish people at times. Never forget the ending of this story and how a man and his family were changed because I was able to deal with my junk. Are you ready to deal with yours? If you allow God to use everything, even your most prized possession, that may result in another life being saved!

6 - One A.M., Waffles, and a Witness

How, then, can they call on the one they have not believed in? And how can they believe in the one of whom they have not heard? And how can they hear without someone preaching to them? And how can they preach unless they are sent? As it is written, "How beautiful are the feet of those who bring good news!"

(Romans 10:14, 15)

I KNOW IT MIGHT SOUND FAR-FETCHED, but the farther along I get in life, the more convinced I become that when times get crazy, there's no doubt God is at the wheel!

I want people always to be prepared for whatever God might bring your way. One of the churches I absolutely love here in Charlotte is Elevation Church. It is the third fastest-growing church in America at the time of this writing. The pastor is only twenty-seven years old. They have four different campuses and have two or three services on each campus reaching an average of about 5,000 to 6,000 people!

Elevation Church is a phenomenal movement of God. Every time I go there, it is a completely different service. You never know what to expect. You never know what kind of video they're going to pull off. You never know what kind of decorations they're going to have to draw you into the service. You never know what the pastor is going to do to make it interesting and impact your heart. You never know what kind of music they're going to be diving into. They do a remarkable job of keeping people on the edge of their seats when it comes to Jesus, and I love that.

The most boring church on the entire planet, in my opinion, is the one you can go to each and every week only to get the same thing, Sunday after Sunday after Sunday. There's nothing exciting going on. It's just the same old stuff.

That is precisely what I love so much about Jesus. When the disciples were walking with their Master, each day was radically different! One day He provided food to feed the masses, the next He healed the leper. One day He was setting a demon-possessed man free, the next He was walking on water. One night He was quieting the storm, the next He was healing someone who was lowered through the roof of a house. One moment, He was arguing with the Pharisees, the next He was driving people out of the temple because they were making His Father's house a den of thieves.

Every day with Jesus had to have been an unforgettable experience, and that's the kind of "anything-can-happen" attitude I want people to have in their hearts day-in and day-out. What a thrill it is to know that Christ is always present and always ready to shake things up through various situations and circumstances and through *your* testimony. I hope to get the point across loud and clear that testifying does not have to be some boring, mechanical item on our checklist that you must get done in order to keep God happy.

The opportunities we have to testify should make our hearts pound with excitement and our minds soar with anticipation. As we mentioned in chapter three, it's critical that we be sober, alert, and in-tune with the Holy Spirit because it is He who will lead us into some of the most random and exciting acts of ministry. In fact, I am positive that crazy circumstances come with the territory of being a Christ-follower. So, be prepared for the unexpected!

For example, let's look at a spur of the moment opportunity in Philip's life from Acts 8 where we read that an Angel of the Lord told Philip to go south to a desert road that led from Jerusalem to Gaza. On his way, Philip saw an Ethiopian eunuch, an important official in charge of the treasury of Candace, queen of the Ethiopians. The man had been to Jerusalem to worship and was sitting in his chariot on his way home, reading the book of Isaiah. That's when "The Spirit told Philip, 'Go to that chariot and stay near it' " (Acts 8:9).

Can you imagine? I'm sure old Phil did a double-take when he heard the Spirit's instruction. It makes me picture myself in the downtown of a busy city with all the traffic blurring by and the Spirit of God saying, "Christian, I want you to stand in the middle of that intersection and when the light turns green, I want you to hold up your hands. I want you to stop traffic and just wait for an opportunity to share with those who are lost about the love of My Son."

I've got to be honest with you, as crazy as I am, I probably wouldn't go down with that. But my point is we need to be prepared to live out whatever God, through His Spirit, calls us to live out.

Led by the Spirit, Philip walked faithfully beside this chariot. He may well have felt uncomfortable because he had no idea who this man was or what he was about. And I can only imagine what the Ethiopian eunuch was thinking. He probably thought, as this stranger walked along side his chariot, that he was about ready to get jacked!

But when he got close enough, Philip overheard the eunuch reading from the book of Isaiah and, led by the Spirit, he asked the man, "Do you understand what you are reading?"

"Well, how could I, unless someone guides me?" the eunuch responded.

What an opportunity! You talk about God kicking open a door!

As it turns out, the man is reading the prophecy of Christ's crucifixion. "Please tell me, of whom does the prophet say this? Of himself, or of someone else?" the eunuch asked Peter.

> *"Then Philip began with that very passage of Scripture and told him the good news about Jesus. As they traveled along the road, they came to some water and the eunuch said, 'Look, here is water. Why shouldn't I be baptized?' And he gave orders to stop the chariot. Then both Philip and the eunuch went down into the water and Philip baptized him."* (Acts 8:35-38)

It says when they came up out of the water, "The Spirit of the Lord snatched Philip away; and the eunuch saw him no more, but went on his way rejoicing. But Philip found himself at Azotus..."

That's how Philip lived his life. He testified. And he didn't look for the easy way or the traditional way of testifying. He looked for any opportunity the Spirit would open up, and he jumped right on them.

Sometimes that's not easy. We need to be alert, flexible, and open enough to notice when the Holy Spirit opens up a creative opportunity to testify. And we need to embrace those moments because we know He's at work rather than run from them because we're scared.

One night several years ago, after I had spoken at Charleston Southern University and stayed late to talk to some of the students, I was hungry and needed to wind down, so I found my way to the local Waffle House.

It was about 12:30 a.m., and there were only about three customers in the restaurant. It was very quiet. So, I took a seat at a booth in the corner, where I ordered a cup of coffee and opened up my Bible.

Within a few minutes, this group of raunchy, rowdy-looking teenagers walks in, at which time I literally said to myself, "Just leave those guys over there, Lord. I don't want to talk to them. I don't want to witness to them. I don't want anything to do with them at this moment. Let me have my time in here. This is my time, *my* way...I've worked all evening. Lord, just leave them way over there."

As I sat chilling in the corner booth, one of the youths, the one who had come in the door first led the group to the table directly beside me. The leader was a huge guy with a twelve-inch purple Mohawk and purple spikes sticking out the sides of his head. His tee shirt read, "I Hate People," and his black leather jacket featured a swastika, the Nazi-fascist symbol. This was one ugly, angry-looking dude; and the guys with him were equally as mean-looking.

"Okay, God, okay," I prayed. "Only You could do this. If you're opening up an opportunity here, if this is a Philip moment, then I'll walk beside the chariot, and I'll be prepared to do whatever you need me to do."

I normally don't listen in on people's conversations, but they were talking about guns, and when people are talking about guns at the Waffle House at 12:30 a.m., you'd better listen up.

"Well, I got me a nine-millimeter," one of them said.

"My .357 blows away that cap gun," said another.

"Yeah, well I got a Kevlar jacket, and nothin' can shoot through it."

"Bull," said one, "I got a rifle with piercing rounds that'll burn holes right through that Kevlar vest."

"I'll throw one of my flash-smoke grenades at you, and you'll be so blind you'll never find me."

"I got me a double-pump shotgun that'll take care of all-ya'll."

Back and forth they went, and I was sitting there thinking, "I can't believe these teenagers have all these weapons! I mean, is this a joke?"

These kids, in their black clothes with their piercings and "Goth" look, kept going back and forth with such intensity that it made me think of the Columbine High School tragedy. I was really paying attention, I mean, getting ready to jump them if they did anything crazy!

As I sat there listening to them, suddenly, up from my stomach, all the way through my chest, out my throat, and through my mouth, I spoke, without even thinking: "Hey, I got something better than all that." It was one of those moments when you think to yourself, *I didn't really just say that, did I?*

The big guy looks at me, slowly takes a hit from his cigarette, and says, "What you got, big boy?"

"Well, let me tell you what I got, big guy," I said. "I know a Man who, when He walked on this earth, He gave the blind their sight. I know a Man who cast demons out of people. I know a man who could touch people and the leprosy would flee from their bodies. I know a Man who loved so much that He was willingly beaten to the point of being unrecognizable. His flesh hung off. His ribs were exposed. He was put on a cross and nailed there so we could have forgiveness of our sins.

"The world, the enemies, and Satan thought they had the victory by putting His cold corpse in the ground. But three days later, He arose from the dead to let us know that we could have victory through His death. And He went and revealed Himself to certain people so that His story would live on. Then He ascended to heaven to be with His Father. And now He sits and He waits to have a love relationship with anyone who would believe and have faith in Him.

"You and your guns can kill people, but me and my Savior can raise them from the dead. That's what I got, Dog. What you got?"

Everyone went silent. The big guy takes another puff, looks around at his friends, and says, "That's pretty good. That's good, man. That's real good." Several of them started laughing. "Guys," I said, "let me share my story with you."

All eyes were on me. All ears were listening. A Hell's Angel-looking biker who was sitting across the room, leaned toward us. Our waitress came over and lingered there. The guy behind the counter, flipping the eggs, began listening. And I just shared my testimony, the very same story I shared in chapter one of this book.

When I paused and looked to my left, one of the teenagers, a small blond-haired boy, was crying. "Son," I said, "I'm here for you tonight." Although I would love to be able to say everyone in the restaurant gave their lives to Christ that night, that did not happen. However, as I saw the tears falling from this one young man's eyes, I told him I felt God had brought me there for him.

"Yes, sir," he said. "I have to be honest with you. I've been hanging out with these guys for a long time. I haven't been living my life right. I walked away from church. I walked away from my mom and dad; my grandparents keep me. I've been locked up and going through some tough times. But when you started talking about Jesus, I knew God had sent you in here for me."

"Can I pray for you to re-dedicate your life to Christ?"

"Yes, sir."

And we prayed, there at the Waffle House at 2 a.m.

"I want you to get up and go home now," I said. "Tell your family what you did. Go find your pastor and tell him the decision you made tonight." Laughing, I said, "And take these guys with the purple hair with you. They need Jesus...we all need Jesus. I want you to be a witness, and I want you to testify about what Christ has done in your life."

He got up. I paid for everybody's food in the whole joint. I praised God for the situation. And everybody left. I got into my truck, drove back to my hotel room, and went to sleep, and I slept in peace. Why? Because I knew that God had given me yet another opportunity to share my faith with someone and a life was changed. I could rest because I had been obedient. And what satisfaction that brings!

Once again, I couldn't have manufactured that moment. It was Spirit-led. I found myself in a crazy situation. Two o'clock in the morning at the Waffle House. Just like Philip and the Ethiopian eunuch. God opened up an incredible opportunity. And who knows what impact that Waffle House chat will have on the others who heard it that night. Seeds were watered in that place. I was obedient.

My challenge to you is, the next "crazy" situation in which you find yourself, don't be uncomfortable, and don't run from it. God can use it; in fact, He designed it. And it has your name written all over it. So, the crazier it is, perhaps the crazier you need to be—for Christ.

Chapter 6
Questions to Dwell On

1) Read **Romans 10:14-15**. It doesn't get more simple than this. According to Philippians 3:5, Paul, who wrote Romans, was an elite part of the tribe of Benjamin, a Hebrew of Hebrews, a Pharisee who was faultless when it came to knowing the Law. But he laid something out for us in Romans 10:14-15, in the simplest of terms. In essence, he said that if we don't live it, how can people see it? If we don't tell it, how can people hear it? How often do you follow this simple command? Is your approach to ministry a legalistic one? Do you go to church on Wednesday and Sunday, dress the part, sing the songs, but don't fulfill the simplest of all passages? Jesus said, "I desire compassion more than sacrifice!"

2) Let's review the story of Philip and the Ethiopian one more time. Read **Acts 8:26-40**. Let's go over the obstacles. One, Philip was a Jew and the Ethiopian was not. Two, Philip came from a simple life with humble circumstances and the Ethiopian served as an important official. Three, Philip was walking into the unknown by obeying the voice of the Spirit. He was also walking alongside the chariot of an important official and literally could have lost his life had God not been in it. Yet, with all these obstacles, Philip still played a part in the Ethiopian's conversion and baptism. Have you ever walked away from the voice of God when He was leading you into Spirit-filled opportunity? What was the thing you feared most?

3) What represents the Waffle House in your life? Are you ready to put aside personal preferences and take the gospel wherever He might lead? If so, your chariot awaits, I assure you!

HERE'S THE JUICE:

No one is asking for you to try to be me. In fact, we each have different gifts and abilities God has given us. We all travel in different circles where God has placed us. The one thing we all do have in common is that, because God has reconciled us, we are to help other people to be reconciled to Him. We are all to be passionate for Christ and to share our faith. I have opportunities to reach the people God puts in my path, and you have totally different opportunities for the people He puts in yours. We all simply need to be ready for the doors He opens for us. Remember my Waffle House story as well as Philip and the Ethiopian and simply be faithful with the opportunities God chooses to give you. I look forward to hearing all the God stories that result from your passionate desire to reach and serve.

7 - Thieves, Thugs, and Angels in Disguise

While Jesus was having dinner at Matthew's house,
many tax collectors and "sinners" came and ate with him
and his disciples. When the Pharisees saw this,
they asked his disciples,
"Why does your teacher eat with tax collectors and 'sinners'?"
On hearing this, Jesus said, "It is not the healthy who need a doctor,
but the sick. But go and learn what this means:
'I desire mercy, not sacrifice.'
For I have not come to call the righteous, but sinners."

(Matthew 9:10–13)

IN MANY WAYS, THE STORY OF THE TAX COLLECTOR, Zacchaeus, rings similar to the story of the tax collector, Matthew, who became one of Christ's disciples. The reason this little man, Zacchaeus, interests me so much is because of the way he met Jesus, and what ultimately happened to him as a result of their meeting.

I hate to be so bold, but I put Zacchaeus in the same category as Matthew. Before they believed in Jesus, they were both basically thieves who robbed innocent people. Matthew was the worst. He was the kind of tax collector who would go to a bridge, claim that bridge, then charge people money to cross it. Zacchaeus was the same breed of cat. Don't let the niceness of how the story turns out fool you.

Before he met Jesus, Zacchaeus was a thief, one who was surely despised by the whole community. Nobody could stand the man because he robbed people "legally" under the guise of "tax collector."

But everything changed that day Jesus passed through Zacchaeus's town of Jericho. The Bible tells us Zacchaeus was one of the chief tax collectors and was very wealthy. Yet, he had a strong curiosity about Jesus.

I think that's something to keep in mind when we meet people. They may be worldly. They may pretend to have no interest whatsoever in us or in our God. But deep down, people without God are hurting puppies. When they see the light, salt, and living water flowing from us, when they see our joy and our interest in them, it makes them thirsty, and they begin to long for what we have.

Zacchaeus was thirsty. He'd heard all about the miracles of Jesus and His radical love. Now, he wanted to see who Jesus was. However, being a short man, he could not see over the other people. So, he ran up ahead of everyone and worked his way up into a sycamore-fig tree and waited for the crowd to sweep his way. And it worked!

Sure enough, Jesus got to that spot with that big branch hanging overhead, and he looked up and said, "Zacchaeus, come down immediately. I must stay at your house today." The Bible says Zacchaeus came down at once and welcomed Him gladly.

> *All the people saw this and began to mutter, "He has gone to be the guest of a 'sinner.'" But Zacchaeus stood up and said to the Lord, "Look, Lord! Here and now I give half of my possessions to the poor, and if I have cheated anybody out of anything, I will pay back four times the amount." Jesus said to him, "Today salva tion has come to this house, because this man, too, is a son of Abraham. For the Son of Man came to seek and to save what was lost."*
>
> (Luke 19:7-10)

I love the story of Jesus eating with Zacchaeus and similar stories about when Christ shared meals and time with sinful people, from Pharisees and "religious" people to obvious sinners like the prostitute and the woman at the well.

In each of those instances, there were always people outside looking through the windows, gasping and gossiping among themselves. "Can you believe Jesus? He's supposed to be the Son of God! Would the Messiah eat with such people? If He were the Messiah, He would be holier than that!"

A lot of churches today open up their doors to a select group of people. The Lutherans might open their doors to the Lutheran way, the Methodists to the Methodist way, the Baptists to the Baptist way, the charismatic movement to the charismatic way, and the Catholic church to the Catholic way. It's sad to me that we don't have just one church with one God and one Savior.

I know that's what we teach, but do we really live it out in our hearts and lives? Jesus was one who broke down those kinds of walls, wall after wall after wall. And He threw many of the "religious" people of the day into confusion because He was one who had no walls. Like Him, we should have no walls. And we should never give special preference to the beautiful and the rich over the poor and downcast.

> *Suppose a man comes into your meeting wearing a gold ring and fine clothes, and a poor man in shabby clothes also comes in. If you show special attention to the man wearing fine clothes and say, "Here's a good seat for you," but say to the poor man, "You stand there" or "Sit on the floor by my feet," have you not discrimi nated among yourselves and become judges with evil thoughts? If you really keep the royal law found in Scripture, "Love your neigh bor as yourself," you are doing right. But if you show favoritism, you sin and are convicted by the law as lawbreakers.*
>
> (James 2:2-4, 8, 9)

A number of years ago, I served as the pastor of a church in a college town. It was an amazing church started by a friend of mine who had ventured to another city to start a new fellowship and left me in charge of teaching and shepherding this vibrant church.

We hosted one Sunday morning service, which usually drew

about 150 people, and there were three Sunday evening services. Throughout the day we ministered to about 750 college students. It was a college-based ministry. Some of the best days of my life were spent during my four years of leadership at that church.

At that time, I was also a regular speaker at a large Christian campus ministry that met at the university every week. With about one thousand students in attendence, itwas one of the biggest college ministry groups in the nation. The first time I went to one of their meetings on campus, I immediately thought, "Man, these are some beautiful people." I got the impression that this was one of the "elite" groups on campus. Popular people. Fraternity guys. Preps. Sorority gals. Intelligent people. Athletes. The Abercrombie & Fitch crowd, for sure. One type of people definitely missing from this crowd was the rough, course-looking type (like me).

Anyway, when I spoke that first time, they seemed to enjoy it, and they invited me back several months later. Very soon, I became a regular speaker there. I was loving the ministry with this group of students, but soon the Lord began to put an extremely heavy burden on my heart about the worldliness and favoritism of this group. Before long, I had the impression that I had been sent to challenge them in these areas and to find out whether, behind all the nice clothes and pretty faces, they were the real deal.

So, after several weeks of planning, I spoke to one of the campus group's leaders, who was also an intern at my church. I talked him into dressing up as a homeless person and doing a spoof on the college kids. We bought a bottle of cheap wine and poured it all over him. I rolled him around in a dumpster and made him wear some wino clothes I purchased at the thrift store. He looked nasty and he smelled even worse. I got a pack of cigarettes, blew smoke all over him, and told him to light up as well.

Once he was completely grungy-looking, and smelling like a cross between a brewery and a tobacco shop, I took him and laid him out on the steps at the entrance of the building where one thousand-plus students would walk past as they entered the campus ministry meeting that night.

Next, I hid in the bushes with my video camera.

During the next unbelievable hour, I filmed as hundreds of young people stepped over this man, looked at him, veered around him, and gathered in crowds all around him just to talk. Not one person asked if he needed help. Not one person asked if he wanted to go into the service with them to hear about Jesus. Not one sought him out to see if he needed money for food or clothes. Not one asked anything. Instead, they looked at him as if he was a spectacle and one who was invading their space, and they went about their business.

After filming all of that, I took my friend downtown and, in the same smelly condition, laid him right outside the door of one of the wildest bars in town. I went off and hid, with my video camera on, and guess what happened?

The first three guys who walked out of that bar got on their hands and knees and asked the "homeless man" if he needed help.

Absolutely amazing.

It lined up exactly like the story of the Good Samaritan. You had a priest and a priest's servant, the supposed "religious" of the day, who walked right on by a man who had been beaten, robbed, stripped of everything he had, and left for dead.

Then a Samaritan comes along, the supposed "unclean" of the day. Here's a guy who is despised by the Jews because he is half Gentile and half Jew. Yet, this despised Samaritan picks this poor victim up, bandages his wounds, takes him to a hotel where he pays to have the man fed, clothed, and cared for. The Samaritan even went so far as to say, "Whatever expense you incur, I will return and pay you back. Please, give the man whatever he needs."

Love without limits.

Boundless, unconditional love.

Did Jesus wait for us to clean up our acts before He went to the cross for us? No. He just loved, even unto death. Shouldn't we do the same?

What good is it, my brothers, if a man claims to have faith but has no deeds? Can such faith save him? Suppose a brother or sister is without clothes and daily food. If one of you says to him, "Go, I wish you well; keep warm and well fed," but does nothing about his physical needs, what good is it? In the same way, faith by itself, if it is not accompanied by action, is dead.

(James 2:14-17)

The very next week I went to preach at my church, where many of the students from that campus ministry attended church. I showed my video there. I also showed it to the president of the campus ministry group and some other students. Let me tell you, I was almost crucified on that campus. As a matter of fact, I have never been invited back to speak at that campus ministry.

Looking back on it, I realize the method by which I attempted to challenge those students was somewhat rudimentary and perhaps bordering on deceptive. However, perhaps we can still learn from it today. After all, what does it mean to be a Christian, a Christ-follower? How can you be genuinely transformed by what Jesus did on the cross and treat any human being with scorn and contempt? Once you have surrendered your life to Christ, your life is not your own anymore; you've been called for a higher purpose. What does that mean?

It means picking that person up on the side of the road who has been hurt and ditched. It means bending down and talking with that guy laying on the steps who looked and smelled so nasty, and helping him, and testifying about Jesus—not only through words but through actions and works of service, like those of the good Samaritan.

John the Baptist said it this way: "He must increase, but I must decrease."

Keep on loving each other as brothers. Do not forget to entertain strangers, for by so doing some people have entertained angels without knowing it. Remember those in prison as if you were their fellow prisoners, and those who are mistreated as if you yourselves were suffering.

(Hebrews 13:1-3)

This is a profound topic in my life because I believe many churches today have walked away from the people like Zacchaeus and from those who are lost. Many of today's churches are all about the clique, but they're not about being God's arms and feet and hands and heart.

If it was all about remarkable buildings, we've accomplished that. If it was about beautiful singing, we've got that right now. If it was about colorful preaching, there are hundreds of charismatic pastors. Let me tell you, we have the most wonderful buildings, recording artists, and pastors right here in America, but we have no great awakenings and no mighty revivals.

Why?

To a great extent I believe it's because our churches are cliquish and so singular in vision that the vision has become all about them! What the church should be doing is equipping the saints to get out of our comfort zones to go out and be Christ to the world—outside the four walls of the church.

Be challenged, my friends, to be on the lookout for the homeless, the downtrodden, the desperate, the despairing. Our testimony must reach beyond the people with whom we are "comfortable," and impact those we would have never imagined Christ would call us to go and reach.

It was encounters like this that the Pharisees hated most. They would have never dreamed that the gospel should go out to someone like Zacchaeus. I guarantee you Zacchaeus was lost, he was a thief, and he was despised. But because this man received the love of Christ and the testimony of what Christ was there to do, Zacchaeus said, "I will pay back double anything that I have robbed from anyone. I will give back everything." This man underwent an amazing transformation. And it all started because Jesus looked up into a tree and decided to share a meal and the story of His life with this man who was in need.

Many churches today have the mentality those people did who walked over and around my friend when he was dressed up like a homeless person. They have beautiful people, smooth preaching, and professional singing, but that's as far as it goes. It doesn't even reach outside the doors to the front steps of where they meet.

I was reading the obituaries in the newspaper the other day (I guess that's how you know when you're getting old), where I read the obituary of one Alvin E. Spencer, Jr., nicknamed "Bud." There was a photograph of him and he looked like a happy fellow with much joy on his face.

The obituary read: "The Reverend Spencer, 84, died Saturday, June 7, 2008. He resided in Georgia, but was a reverend and retired Baptist missionary who grew up in Charlotte. He served in the U.S. Marine Corp during World War II and later served as a missionary in Okinawa, Japan, for 43 years, beginning in 1952."

How about that?

Here was a man who fought the Japanese in World War II, yet later in life, went to that very land of Okinawa, Japan, to share the story of Christ's love. He was there much of his life. He received the gift of salvation God had given him, then set out to make a difference in the lives of others.

Thank God for men and women like the Reverend Alvin E. "Bud" Spencer, Jr.

Indeed, that's when you know you've had a transformation—when you are willing to share your story and do something radical, and testify, even to the people with whom you were once cold-blooded enemies.

May we do the same.

Chapter 7
Questions to Dwell On

1) Read **Matthew 9:10-13**. I love this scripture about Matthew and the story of Zacchaeus. Both men were despised by the poor because they were swindlers. The rich hated them because of the way they gained their wealth. There was no nobility; they were simply thieves. Yet Jesus found value in both men and salvation was next in order. Who sits next to you in the pew on Sunday? Who sips Starbucks next to you while the latest Chris Tomlin or David Crowder worship song plays to a room full of candles at your college ministry? Last but not least, who stands in the game room chomping chips and sipping a Mountain Dew at your youth ministry? If they don't look something like Matthew or Zacchaeus did before they found Christ, perhaps you and your church are focusing on the wrong people. Remember, "It's not the healthy who need a doctor, but the sick."

2) Read **Luke 19:1-10**. What was the main obstacle for Zacchaeus to overcome before receiving Jesus in his heart? Sadly enough it was the church of the day. Notice how those standing around were complaining that Jesus went to be with a sinner. Only church people talk like that. Is your heart open to do ministry with those the church would leave on the front steps? It very well might come down to you leading the way in making a difference.

3) Read **James 2:14-17**. Martin Luther, the leader of the Great Reformation, wanted the book of James thrown out of the Bible because he felt it would mislead people into thinking they needed to work their way into heaven. Far from the truth. James was writing the obvious, if you say you love Jesus, and are filled with the Holy Spirit, then there will automatically be works that follow. What good would it be for me to tell my wife I love her but then go out and cheat? I promise you my wife would not feel very loved. If we say we are in love with Jesus then we will be bearing fruit that represents that kind of love relationship. If we're not, maybe we need to take some time to get alone with God and re-examine our love for Him. Ask Him to set our hearts on fire again with love for Him and love for the lost, like the homeless man on the steps of the church.

HERE'S THE JUICE:

The world is full of Matthews and Zacchaeuses, and they will stay right where they are unless we take Christ to them. In the story of the college ministry, I couldn't have made it any easier for them to be the hands of Christ extended, yet they still chose the selfish path. Once you give your life to Christ, you step from a life of being served to a life of serving others. Many people in the church today have a hard time accepting that philosophy. They think the church is all about them instead of what they can offer others in need. Are you that type of Christian? If you are, it's about time for a change, wouldn't you say?

8 - Who Has Bewitched You?

I am astonished that you are so quickly deserting
the one who called you by the grace of Christ
and are turning to a different gospel —
which is really no gospel at all.
Evidently some people are throwing you into
confusion and are trying to pervert the gospel of Christ.
But even if we or an angel from heaven should preach
a gospel other than the one we preached to you,
let him be eternally condemned! As we have already said,
so now I say again: If anybody is preaching to you
a gospel other than what you accepted,
let him be eternally condemned!

(Galatians 1:6-9)

BEWARE! THERE ARE MANY DIFFERENT RELIGIONS and legalistic people out there who will approach devout Christians in an attempt to steal, kill, and destroy what Christ has done in our lives. That is why it is so vitally important that we know the Word, know our enemy, cling to the miracles God's worked in our lives, understand the power we have in Christ, and continue to share our testimonies until Christ calls us home.

At one time in his life, the apostle Paul went on a missionary journey to Galatia. Later, he wrote a letter to friends he had made there, which we now know as the book of Galatians. Unlike many of his letters, Paul gives only a brief greeting to the Galatians and quickly launches into his point, which he writes to "all the brothers with me" (and this is my paraphrase): "Guys, you need to be on your game! Your testimony is shattered right now. You're losing the grip on your faith. You've walked away from your first love and from what Christ has called you to do and from how He has called you to live.

"Through other people, the enemy—Satan—is deceiving you. He's causing you to question the salvation you received by faith alone. He wants you to think there are other things you need to do, like be circumcised, in order to be true believers. That is a false and perverted gospel! Don't fall for it! Whose approval are you trying to win? Men's or God's?"

> *You foolish Galatians! Who has bewitched you? Before your very eyes Jesus Christ was clearly portrayed as crucified. I would like to learn just one thing from you: Did you receive the Spirit by observing the law, or by believing what you heard? Are you so foolish? After beginning with the Spirit, are you now trying to attain your goal by human effort?*
>
> (Galatians 3:1-3)

We have something that no human being can refute or takeaway, and that is our God-stories and the faith that God has put into our hearts. In his letter to the Galatians, Paul urges them to do an about-face so their testimony will continue to shine and have the value and power it was intended to have. I am urging you to do the same today.

A poll taken not long ago stated that the number one reason unbelievers don't give their lives to Christ is because they believe most Christians are hypocrites who don't live what they claim to believe.

It is critical that our lives and consciences be pure and that we walk with Jesus Christ minute-by-minute so that our testimonies have power. In addition, we need to be aware, as Paul warned the church of Galatia, that there are people and organizations out there—like the Mormon church, Jehovah's Witnesses, the Bahá'í faith, the Muslim religion, Scientologists, and others—who want to destroy our faith and our testimony based on man-made traditions, legalism, lies, and false gods. It is up to God's true followers to testify the real-deal Jesus so people can have genuine, eternal life-change.

This whole issue came to life for me several years ago when I came home one day and saw a Latino man named Juan working on the tile in our kitchen.

Now, let me stop right here and tell you clearly that I am a person who is driven by new relationships. I have always had that ADHD personality that just causes me to be wide-open, going 100 mph all the time. In fact, if I could just meet a new person every five or ten minutes, I would get all the energy and "high" my body would need to remain physically and mentally strong, and I wouldn't have to worry about vitamins, diet, or exercise.

So, new relationships are what really motivate me. My wife, Amy, is just the opposite. If a stranger tried to come up and introduce himself or herself to Amy out of the blue, she would shut up and lock down, I guarantee it. She is a quadruple introvert while I'm a quadruple extrovert.

When Amy and I were about to start a church-plant at a movie theater in Charlotte, the people funding the new church sent us to a marriage counseling retreat center in the North Carolina mountains. They wanted us to go through seven days of marriage counseling to make sure our relationship was in tip-top condition before we attempted to plant a new church.

When we arrived at the facility, we gathered with all of the other church-planting couples for dinner to meet the man who ran the facility and who was going to be counseling us. At age sixty-five or seventy, he was retired and had a slew of degrees that made him very knowledgeable about people and about getting them ready for church-planting.

He let us know we would be working with some young counselors during the week and that we would conclude by working with him at the close of the week. He proceeded to introduce us to our counselor, a phenomenal guy with a sweet spirit. His name was Richard.

We all sat down for dinner and the elderly man who oversaw the facility kept asking me question after question after question. I just kept answering. Although it seemed like I may have been dominating the conversation, I was simply answering his questions as I became more and more excited about the church plant, meeting all the new people at the retreat, and sharing my story and testimony.

The next day Richard came up to me and said, "Christian, there's something I want to talk to you about. We need to start you on medication."

"Medication?" I said. "What are you talking about?"

He told me the elderly man who ran the facility had diagnosed me with ADHD. "He's determined that you lack focus and that you talk too much and that you have too much energy. You get too excited. The medicine will help you remain a bit calmer and keep your composure. It's not a large dosage."

"You're kidding me, right?" I said. "He wants me to start medication? What kind?"

Richard named the medication and said, "You can start on it today."

I've got to tell you, I almost blew a gasket.

"Richard," I said through clenched teeth, "I want *you* to focus right now; focus in on my eyes. Are you focused in?"

"Yeah," Richard said.

"You tell that old man when I'm ready to come up here and give up my life, and sit on a couch, and counsel people for the rest of my days, then I'll come get some of his medicine," I said. "But until then, I don't want you to mention that again. Jesus never told Peter to get on medication. So, I'm going to let my story be heard. I'm going to testify. I'm going to get excited about new relationships. And even if I am a loud mouth at times, I'm going to be loud-mouthing it about my Lord and Savior."

My wife and I still have a good laugh about that. She actually looked at Richard after I had finished and said, "Now you know what

I've had to be married to all these years."

Anyway, back to coming home to the Latino man, Juan, working in my kitchen. I'll never forget the feeling I had when I came home. More than being excited about getting new tile, I was psyched that I was going to have a chance to witness to this man

"How you doing?" I asked.

I quickly figured he didn't understand me as he tilted his head and just smiled and nodded. Thinking fast, I called a Spanish-speaking pastor friend of mine in Charlotte and said, "Dude, you gotta teach me a couple quick lines of Spanish. I got a Latino man in my kitchen, and I want to witness to him."

As I explained more, my pastor buddy got excited and said, "Man, come on over, I'll teach you a couple things real fast."

I went over to his place and spent about an hour with him. He gave me a Latino Bible and taught me two or three sentences. So, I took off back to the house, walked in the door, and my wife said, "Where have you been?"

"Check this out, baby," I said. "You're going to love this."

I looked at Juan and said, in Spanish, "Hello, how are you?"

He looked at me and, in Spanish, said something like, "I'm doing fine."

"What is your name?" I asked in Spanish.

He told me his name was Juan, and I told him my name.

I was getting so excited, and my wife was looking pretty impressed.

"This is awesome," I said to Amy. "Check this out."

In Spanish, I said, "I have a gift for you. It is the Word of God."

This guy stands up with a blank look, comes over, and gets right in my face. I didn't know whether he was going to hug me, kiss me, hit me, or what he was going to do. But, he looked right into my eyes and said, "Man, thanks anyway, but I'm a Mormon."

I was flabbergasted.

The only thing I could muster was, "Yeah, and you speak perfect

English, too!"

He looked right at me and said, "Yeah, and I'm a Mormon."

"Dude, why didn't you tell me you could speak English?" I said. "I just messed up like a whole couple hours of my day trying to learn your language. You could have saved me a lot of time."

I made myself calm down. "Well, listen," I held out the Spanish Bible, "here's a Bible for you, anyway."

"Nah," he rejected the Book with an outstretched hand. "I don't need the Bible."

I said, "Juan, I've got to ask you, why are you a Mormon? Don't you realize that the founder of the Mormon Church, Joseph Smith, said he found some tablets on his grandfather's farm. Doesn't that sound a little fishy to you?"

"No, no, it doesn't sound fishy to me," he said. "I believe that an angel brought him those tablets."

"Yeah, but don't you understand that the Scriptures say that Satan masquerades as an angel of light? Don't you realize that in the book of Galatians, Paul said that if an angel or another person or anyone preaches another gospel other than the one I'm giving you right now, that person will be eternally condemned to hell?

"I don't doubt Joseph Smith may have gotten his hands on some tablets," I said, "but I don't think they came from an angel of the Lord. I believe it was an angel of evil, and that Satan produced that angel to build a lie which millions and millions of people are giving their eternity over to."

He stared at me with a far off look, as if he was simply listening to be polite.

"Do you understand that Joseph Smith had eleven disciples and that he stayed away from having twelve because he didn't want to take the chance he'd end up with someone like Judas in his group? What does that tell you, right there? Plus, of those eleven disciples, eight signed a document before they died saying Joseph Smith was a fake and a liar; the other three were killed in a gunfight in Utah. Those are the eleven disciples Joseph Smith chose. Why in the world would you invest your eternity in that?"

"I'll tell you why," Juan said as this incredible look of intensity hardened on his face. "When I arrived in this country, I went to every church that you could imagine." He went through and named denomination after denomination. "I went to church after church after church. No one received me. No one would build a relationship with me. No one would invite me to home groups or Bible studies. They did not ask me to get connected with them. I felt like an outcast.

"Right about that time, I was out of work and about to lose my house. My children despised me and did not respect me. My wife was about to leave me. Then, two Mormons showed up at my house on bicycles. They taught me how to have a relationship with the lord. They discipled my children and taught them how to respect their father. They counseled my wife, and she fell back in love with me. They actually made my house payment until I could make it again. They found me work. *That* is why I'm a Mormon. These people came in and transformed my entire family. I didn't get that at any of those other churches but from two guys on bikes who lived out what they believed."

It hit me hard. I had tears in my eyes. It broke my heart, and I apologized to him. He had been won over by acts of service. Granted, the foundation of those deeds was not Christ, the Cornerstone. But the acts themselves were good enough to draw Juan into their fellowship. There was basically nothing else I could share with him because he had been so impacted by these two Mormons on bikes and the Mormon Church. So, I prayed for him. And I think about him occasionally.

But you know what? That episode dealt me a strong and sobering challenge, and I extend that challenge to you. We need to live strong and testify with the message that Christ has put in our lives. Because, if we're not doing it, just like at the church of Galatia, someone will come in to steal, kill, and destroy.

Paul had given them the real-deal Jesus and some awesome things had happened. He went where God led him and heard about what was going on in Galatia—that they had done an about-face and completely walked away from what they had learned.

Paul challenged them. "Who came in and taught you this false gospel?"

There are many churches today whose people do not go out and present the real-deal Jesus to a hungry world, but He is what they need. If we don't make sure that we are testifying about who Jesus is and what He has done in our lives, and share our stories, then we can guarantee that someone else will share another message. It may be two guys on bicycles, or Muslims, or Jehovah's Witnesses, or Scientologists, or just the world, pulling people into worldliness rather than into God's kingdom of light.

You and I, God's children, are *constantly* on the battlefield. If we give Satan any room, even just a slight foothold, he can invade our hearts and minds like poison and destroy not only our lives but our testimonies. If that happens, the people who we were meant to reach will never be impacted for Christ.

Not long ago, my wife was reading me a story from the *Charlotte Observer* about a professor from a large, well-respected university in the south. He is a best-selling author and was once a self-declared born-again Christian. The article blew me away. Here is a man who was once a Christian and, while working on his doctorate degree at a prestigious university, ended up denouncing his faith in Christ.

No longer does he believe that God's will is His will or that His Word is His Word. And guess what? This man is the leading religion professor at the well-known university he represents. His classes are some of the most popular on campus, and for one of the classes, there is a two-year waiting list to get in.

The reporter who wrote the story watched the professor autograph books at a recent book signing and wrote that he was an arrogant fellow who outwardly talked down to Christians and openly bashed Christianity. He actually begins his class by asking his students to raise their hands if they believe the Bible is the genuine word of God. Then he asks, "Who reads the Bible?" When only a few hands go up he says, "That proves my point. The very Bible many of you said you believe, few of you actually read, or study, or live out."

Men and women like this professor, who I feel safe to call antichrists, are attempting to make similar proclamations all over the world.

> *But there were also false prophets among the people, just as there will be false teachers among you. They will secretly in troduce destructive heresies, even denying the sovereign Lord who bought them—bringing swift destruction on themselves. Many will follow their shameful ways and will bring the way of truth into disrepute.*
>
> (2 Peter 2:1, 2)

I would love to debate this man. I would let him have it. Actually, I'd prefer to do a celebrity boxing match with him. I do believe I would tear his head up because he constantly attacks my God and His people. I know I'm supposed to love the man, but I get so intense and aggressive and heated when I hear about guys like this ruining whole households and turning young and impressive minds against God.

If I had this man in front of me right now, I would tell him my God-story, about when I surrendered my life to Christ on I-85, and how God made that amazing thing happen. I would tell him some of the other stories in this book, and he could not refute any of it. Why? Because, they are my stories. They happened to me. They are my miracles. They transformed me. Nothing can ever separate me from those truths.

If you have a God-story, He wants you to use it, share it, and transform it into something beautiful that multiplies and bears much good fruit. We need to go do battle against these other so-called religions and gods and faiths. Love them? Yes! We invite them into our home and my wife cooks for them. We build friendships and witness to them. We share our God-stories with them. And we watch and wait and keep watering those seeds until God begins to draw them into His kingdom.

> *They overcame him by the blood of the Lamb and by the word of their testimony; they did not love their lives so much as to shrink from death.*
>
> (Revelation 12:11)

Chapter 8
Questions to Dwell On

1) Read **Galatians 1:6-9**. How many times have you seen someone give his or her life to Christ only to fall away shortly thereafter because of temptation and the influence of others? If you're like me, your answer was probably "quite often." That is why it is so important that we make it our life goal to live for Christ, to share the gospel, and to protect the flock as a shepherd would against attacking wolves.

2) Read **2 Peter 2:1-2**. Too often, we fail to spot the attack of the enemy. We get tricked. We become deceived. Why? Because Satan masquerades as an angel of light. We must keep our guard up and be prepared for the attack of the enemy at all times. The number one thing Satan wants to do once we have given our lives to Christ is to kill, steal, and destroy—to ruin our testimony. So be on guard. What precautions do you take to keep the world and false prophets from stealing your zeal and watering down your walk with Jesus?

3) Read **Revelation 12:11**. You know what Satan hates most? A crazy Jesus freak who cares nothing about his own life but is all about laying his life down for God. Stay on guard, watch over the flock, and make a difference to those with whom you come in contact. If you don't, you never know what false doctrine they will be exposed to while waiting on the truth.

HERE'S THE JUICE:

You and I can't do anything about Juan now except pray. But there are many others in the world like Juan who have been hurt, have needs, and are ready for a life change. It's up to us to share the gospel with them and make sure they don't succumb to the lies of the enemy. Do you recognize when the enemy comes to steal, kill, and destroy your testimony? Do you love your life so much that you have walked away from the call to share your faith with those like Juan? Are you ready to lay it all on the line and *testify*?

9 - Breathe Out

All Scripture is God-breathed and is useful for teaching, rebuking, correcting and training in righteousness, so that the man of God may be thoroughly equipped for every good work.

(2 Timothy 3:16, 17)

I LOVE IT THAT EVERY TIME WE READ GOD'S WORD we are actually taking in the deep, rich breath of God! Isn't that a beautiful picture?

I was speaking at a church one time and noticed a humongous Latino dude with tattoos all across his arms and neck. Someone told me he was a visitor who had struggled with crack cocaine. I called him up front, and he got this look on his face as if to say, *Uh, oh. What did I do?*

"All right, big boy," I said. "I want you to breathe in, and I want you to hold that breath as long as you can, okay?"

"Okay." He took an enormous breath—I mean, his big chest was totally pumped up. As he did it, I quoted the above scripture from 2 Timothy 3:16, 17. His face was turning red. He was about to lose it.

"Don't exhale!" I yelled. "Hold it in."

He kept holding it, he kept holding it; everybody was laughing as he turned different shades of red and purple.

"Okay," I patted him, "now, go ahead and breathe out."

He breathed out this enormous breath of air and almost collapsed. More laughter.

"Now, let me ask you, what would have happened if you hadn't breathed out?" I asked.

"Man, I would have died."

The place cracked up.

"That's right," I said. "That's because breathing is a two-way process. You breathe in and you breathe out. According to the Word of God, all Scripture is God-inspired; it is actually God-breathed. So we take in the breath and truth and very mind of God when we read the Bible. But as we inhale this breath of God, if we don't exhale, and tell our stories, and testify into peoples' lives and live-out the new life we've been given, then people die. Do you get me? Unless people hear and see the story and glory of Christ lived out through our lives, they die."

> *I told you that you would die in your sins; if you do not believe that I am the one I claim to be, you will indeed die in your sins."*
>
> (John 8:24)

Just like breathing, our testimonies are a two-way street. Not only do we inhale by receiving Christ and surrendering our lives to Him, but we also exhale by testifying into other peoples' lives. I'm sorry to say, however, that a lot of people don't do that. It's almost as if they are selfish with the gospel. Or they simply choose to occupy their time with other things which, in their eyes, are more important than testifying.

Since we're focusing on air and breath, have you ever thought about how much pollution and toxins you breathe in each time you inhale? They say that the toxins from jets, trains, cars, nuclear energy, and industrial plants is completely ruining the air we take in. Similarly, quite often, people do not breathe in the real breath of God. They do not inhale the powerful stories we've been given to tell.

Years ago, I received a call from the president of the student body at university in the South. "Christian," she said, "I've heard that you are a well-respected speaker and that, in fact, you've spoken on our campus before. We'd love for you to come and be part of an upcoming debate we'll be hosting."

Once again, my ADHD kicked into high gear. "Oh, sure, I'd love it!" I accepted the invitation without even thinking twice about it and without asking any questions. "Let's do it! Let's do it!" I said.

I showed up on campus not even knowing what the debate was about. The crowd was enormous. The auditorium was completely packed. It turned out this was going to be some kind of cultural event for the community, and students got credit for being there. So they were out in full-force because it provided them a chance to hear a debate and get a free grade.

I got up there in front of this packed house, shook hands with several people, and sat down in front of a nameplate on which were written the words, "Reverend Christian Chapman" (the "reverend" part of which always makes me uncomfortable).

Sipping my water, I nodded at three ladies on my left, followed by a gentleman just beyond them. I tried to shake hands with several of them but got a rather cold response. Then, looking out at the packed crowd, at their faces and clothes and mannerisms, I just clearly sensed that I was sitting before a staunch, liberal, left-wing bunch. In fact, I would smile and nod at people in the crowd and got zero response.

Now I was starting to get a bit uncomfortable.

What on earth is this thing all about? I began to wonder.

"Welcome," a female moderator appeared before the crowd with a microphone. "We would like to thank you for coming to tonight's debate, which will focus on homosexuality and non-traditional lifestyles versus Christianity."

As the introductions were given, I quickly found out that the three women next to me were lesbians, the man beside them was an evolutionist, and I had stepped into a raging hornet's nest. My face turned red hot.

I hadn't prepared. What kind of testimony was I going to be? The only resource I had with me was my Bible.

From the start, that predominantly left-wing, gay-rights, evolutionist crowd screamed obscenities at me. The lesbians assured us that the churches and pastors in town embraced them. One even said she attended a popular denominational church in town where the pastor told her that as long as she was in a love relationship, she was fine. Love was what mattered.

I scanned the crowd, practically in disbelief over the pure, outright rebellion displayed before me. The woman to my left, it turned out, was called upon by high school guidance counselors to come speak with troubled students in hopes of helping them determine if, perhaps, they might be hiding "the fact" that they were gay. In other words, the guidance counselor was implying to students that, "I'm going to have you talk to this lady about your troubles because—you know what?—you might be gay."

In fact, the whole front row of the crowd was full of students whom this lady had counseled and infected with the lie that they were homosexual and had encouraged them that that was the way they needed to live their lives. It literally brought tears to my eyes, yet it infuriated me at the same time.

On many campuses across America, I am not even allowed to mention the name of Jesus Christ. Yet, here was this woman whose paying job was to go into schools and testify about what she believed, which was basically the lie that most of these students' emotional problems could be attributed to "the fact" that they were homosexuals whose "true inner self" was being stifled by society and the church.

Several people in the crowd yelled, "Tell us about Sodom and Gomorrah!" "Tell us about how God hates gays!"

"Well, let's talk about Sodom and Gomorrah," I tried to calm them. "In the Scriptures, it says that if God found fifty righteous people, He wouldn't destroy the city. Then thirty, then twenty, then He went all the way down to just ten righteous people. God said, "If you find me ten righteous people, I will not destroy this city. But even just ten righteous people could not be found, so He was forced to bring His wrath.

"That is a God of love," I said among the screams. "That is a God of compassion. He was so willing to save the city that if He could find just ten righteous people, He would spare it. That's how much God loves and cares for people. He is always wanting, longing to offer us a different way of life. But sometimes people just choose their own way, and that's when they bring destruction upon themselves."

The crowd screamed in opposition. Even the female moderator, who was a gay professor on campus and was supposed to be neutral, yelled, "The Bible says not to cast the first stone and here you are casting stones at everybody!"

"I'm not casting stones at anybody," I argued. "I'm just telling people that God loves them, and that He has another way for them to live, and that they need to repent of their sins. I'm not casting stones."

"Yes, you are!" she yelled.

"Do you know where in the Bible it says 'not to cast the first stone'?" I asked. "You probably don't because you've probably never actually read it. It's in John 8, and Jesus actually saved the woman's life by offering her forgiveness and grace. He said, 'None of these people have condemned you and neither do I. Go now and leave your life of sin.' Repent! He brought words of life to her. I'm not here to bring words of death, but words of life."

The crowd booed and hissed. I thought of the crucifixion when all they could yell was, "Crucify Him! Crucify Him!"

My level of intensity increased when I spotted this one young girl in the crowd, to my left, her eyes brimming with tears. She kept looking at me. I watched her for some time. She did not take her watery eyes off mine. It was as if she was speaking to me with those hurting eyes. *When are you going to tell them what needs to be said? When are you going to give them the truth? You have told them God loves them—they know that. They're not responding to that. When are you going to speak truth, even if it hurts?*

Those eyes penetrated my heart and I rose up.

"I've got something to say."

"You need to be quiet," said the woman to my left.

"No, you need to be quiet," I said. "I want to read Scripture." And I read this:

> *Do you not know that the wicked will not inherit the kingdom of God? Do not be deceived: Neither the sexually immoral nor idola ters nor adulterers nor male prostitutes nor homosexual offenders nor thieves nor the greedy nor drunkards nor slanderers nor swindlers will inherit the kingdom of God.*
>
> (1 Corinthians 6:9, 10)

Boos rang out. The mob grew angrier.

"Look," I reasoned, "I found myself in some of these very sins, but when I did, I repented. I tried to live my life in a way that's pleasing to the One who created me. But I received the love and forgiveness of Jesus Christ because I bowed down in humility, admitted my sin, and repented. The problem is you guys won't admit homosexuality is a sinful way of life. But Paul said it clearly, 'If you are a homosexual offender, you will not inherit the kingdom of God.'"

They cursed at the top of their lungs. I was afraid they were going to start throwing things. We continued to go around and around for three hours. It was so frustrating because their anger and intensity never let up. But through it all, I believe I did what God had called me to do.

At the end, the moderator, who was crying, came up and cursed me. "Look, I just stood up for what God called me to stand up for," I said. "I have a right to my opinion and you have a right to yours." She received none of it.

I went home and cried with my wife until 3 a.m. She assured me that I had done what I was supposed to do. "Sometimes, Christian, we obey God and the results, the good fruits, are not immediately evident." I was deeply saddened because I truly loved those people and realized they were on the wide road, along with a lot of other people, leading to eternity in hell.

> *"Enter through the narrow gate. For wide is the gate and broad is the road that leads to destruction, and many enter through it. But small is the gate and narrow the road that leads to life, and only a few find it."*
>
> (Matthew 7:13, 14)

The next day I happened to be back on campus, taking care of some advertising that needed to be posted about a college ministry event at which I would speak the following weekend. So, I decided to hand out drinks to the students and tell them about the event, called Fusion.

As I was handing out the drinks, three young men approached me. They each took a drink, and I invited them to come to Fusion. "No. We were there last night at the debate," one of them said. "We're part of the gay community."

"Okay, man, look we're not going to rehash..."

"No, you don't understand," another said. "We want to apologize to you."

"Apologize to me? Why?" I said.

"We want to apologize about the way some of the people from the gay community treated you. They were hateful. We don't agree with everything you said, but we want to thank you for standing up and telling your story and standing up for what you believe in because churches all over this city will not stand up and confront us. We don't find any power in that or stability. They're cowards. They won't stand up for what they believe in."

Another chimed in, "We just want you to know we believe that you love us and we believe God loves us. Even though we're not willing or ready to accept everything you said, we've agreed to search. So, thank you for speaking out."

I don't know about you, but I thought that was awesome. It made my day, my week, my month! It really opened my eyes and threw out a new challenge in my life. It showed me that sometimes, even though the gospel or testimony or story I share may not be received well, there is still true power going out every time I do!

> *"So is my word that goes out from my mouth: It will not return to me empty, but will accomplish what I desire and achieve the pur pose for which I sent it."*
>
> (Isaiah 55:11)

God's Word is powerful and useful and cuts like a knife when it comes to teaching, rebuking, correcting, and training for righteousness. We need to be out there teaching people and rebuking people who are living sinful lives, but we need to do it in a loving way.

> *Be wise in the way you act toward outsiders; make the most of every opportunity. Let your conversation be always full of grace, seasoned with salt, so that you may know how to answer every one.*
>
> (Colossians 4:5, 6)

Why must we stand up for that which we believe and testify about regarding what sin looks like? Because the Word of God has been so utterly and shamefully watered down, diluted, and distorted. Three girls at that debate told me they went to churches all over town, but the pastors were not teaching the truth because they were scared of confrontation.

Christians should not be out to please man, but God. You don't have to be a pastor to testify, just someone who loves God, realizes what He's done for you, and is led by His Spirit. Confrontation may come when you testify. It may not always be pretty. There may even be persecution. But know this, there is true power from God going out, breathing out, and you never know the eternal difference you might make in someone's life.

I found out the day after the debate that I had made a difference in at least three peoples' lives—those three young men. But even if I hadn't had that conversation with them, I still could have had faith. Faith in what? Faith in the fact that, whenever I testify, stand up, and share my story in boldness, lives will be changed. And the same goes for you.

Chapter 9
Questions to Dwell On

1) Read **2 Timothy 3:16**. Take the breathe-in, breathe-out test so you will know how this scripture is supposed to work. Take a deep breath and hold it in as long as you can. At the moment you find yourself desperate for air you will get a picture of the world and its desperation to receive the breath of God. The word of God was never meant to be kept a secret but was given to let the world know who God is and how life can be new with Him at its core. There are several questions we need to cover before you are ready to breathe life into others.

2) Do you know the word of God? How can you tell others what you don't know yourself? And how can you give others what you don't have? Read the temptation of Jesus in **Matthew 4:1-11**. What was the key to Jesus' victory? It was simply the word of God. That is our most powerful and destructive weapon when it comes to defeating the enemy of the battlefield. The Bible is our guide as we walk through this thing called life. Quite simply, the word of God is the breath of God that gives us life.

3) Could you defend your faith if you were attacked as I was at Winthrop University? Read **1 Peter 3:15**. I see many Christians today living weak faith because they are unprepared for battle. They receive Christ and take up the armor of God, but as life goes on they wander further and further from the front line. Having the victory is more than just knowing the word but living it out. One might argue that knowledge is most important, but no one can argue with a life lived passionately in blind faith. Let the world see your love relationship with Jesus on a daily basis.

HERE'S THE JUICE:

Whether you realize it or not, you are on the battlefield. Now it's time to be prepared to fight for the One you say you love and serve. One of my favorite documentaries is Band of Brothers, the true story about the 101st Airborne in World War II. The beginning of this documentary featured testimonies from the actual men who fought in the 101st Airborne. One of the men said in his hometown, everyone signed up for the war; no one had to be drafted. There were only four who didn't make it because of physical disabilities; all four committed suicide because they weren't able to serve their country. "It was a different time," he said. Why did these men commit suicide? It wasn't because of a lack of passion or their desire to make a difference for the cause of freedom. It wasn't because they didn't want to go or that they would be cowards under fire. It was because the military felt they weren't prepared, nor could they get them prepared, for what they would experience in the face of war. Please don't let that be your Christian walk. We have enough walking dead in the church without adding to the body count. *Be prepared!*

10 - Least of These

But you will receive power when the Holy Spirit comes on you;
and you will be my witnesses in Jerusalem,
and in all Judea and Samaria,and to the ends of the earth.

(Acts 1:8)

JUST THINK, THOSE WERE JESUS' VERY LAST WORDS before he was taken up into heaven. In some versions of the Bible it reads "remotest parts of the earth" instead of "ends of the earth." That word "remotest" actually means the "lowliest" places. I think we know who hangs out at the lowliest places on earth—it's the lowliest people of our world.

It's not up to us to be selective about who we testify to. We can't just say, "Well I'm going to testify to this group of friends," or, "I'm only going to share my testimony with people who look like me, dress like me, and have the same amount of money as me."

If you want to be successful sharing your testimony, you need to begin searching out the lowest places on earth and testifying to the people who live there.

Recently, I was leading a Bible study in Kings Mountain, North Carolina, when several young people expressed their frustration about sharing their testimonies with their friends only to be rejected.

"Have you ever witnessed to a homeless person?" I asked. "Have you ever tried sharing the gospel with someone who has nothing?" Keep in mind, I'm not talking about the rich young ruler of the Bible to whom Jesus offered eternal life and a chance to walk with Him if he would just sell all he had and follow Jesus. That young man ended up walking away sad. He had so much "stuff" he didn't feel like he needed Jesus; he was more in love with his junk than he was with God or with the notion of having a relationship with His Son.

As I challenged those kids at Kings Mountain, I challenge you now: if you really want to bear much good fruit for God, start looking for the lowest person on earth. Start looking for those who have dire needs and a strong desire for something better in life.

I make it a point to share my faith almost daily and, believe me, I am rejected often. However, I can tell you this, I have never been rejected by a homeless person. Likewise, I have never been rejected when I've driven to downtown Charlotte to help a woman who's called me to say that she can't find her husband and thinks he's holed up in some drug house smoking a crack pipe. I've gone and picked up people like that, I've witnessed to them and to the crack dealers, and none of those people have ever rejected the testimony I've laid on them.

Find people who are truly in the lowest places on earth. Those people are hungry, they are desperate, and they are in need of the Great Physician. Remember, Jesus said he didn't come for those who are healthy but for those who need a doctor. And those people, those patients, can be found in the lowliest places on earth.

Lowly people have a repentant heart because they know that what they *have* is not what they *need*. They realize they have been searching for contentment and peace and joy in smoke and mirrors and lies. They realize they need something bigger, something better—a Savior.

I recently attended an event known as TH3, a conference hosted by Elevation Church, which, as I mentioned in chapter six, is the third fastest-growing church in America. The event was held at the amazing and beautiful Anne R. Belk Theater in downtown Charlotte. This was a really cool place. I mean, I showed up, and there were all these really hip-looking people walking around in their designer jeans and shirts with the retro hair and contemporary shoes. And I've got to tell you, I was blown away by the way I was treated there.

"Christian, welcome, we've been watching for you," said a young lady who approached me and ended up serving as my personal assistant for the day. "Let me give you my cell phone number, and if you need anything at all today, you give me a call, and I'll be there for you." I've never had that happen at all the events I've ever been to. Just to know that that person was personally assigned to me and was there to assist. What a special feeling.

The speakers that day were passionate and they had all kinds of creative ideas about church planting and reaching lost people. At the lunch break, my "personal assistant" found me and handed me a nice sack lunch. She just kept following me around, asking if I needed anything. I was blown away by the "customer service," if you will.

Returning to the conference that afternoon, we were given a bunch of free gifts, including a free computer thumb-drive that you could plug into the USB port on your computer and have access to everything the team at Elevation Church knows about church-planting—and that's a lot.

I got a free TH3 notebook, free pens, books, and other giveaways. One of the things we received was a lime green bag from Just Fresh foods. When I first saw the rather feminine green bag I told my personal assistant I'd rather not carry it. But when she told me it contained some food, I said, "Give me that." A six-foot, 230-pound man never turns down a meal, even if it is health food. And besides, I'm married with three kids, and don't get a lot of free stuff these days, so I was pumped.

After the conference, I was leaving the Belk Theater in downtown Charlotte, and I was just basking in the moment. I'd hung out with all of these beautiful, elite people. I'd received bags of great gifts. I'd sat under the teaching of some of the finest teachers in the country. And then I started seeing homeless people. They were wandering around everywhere. And you know what each one of them was carrying? One of those feminine lime green bags from Just Fresh.

It almost brought me to my knees.

During lunch, some of the leaders from Elevation Church had taken their Just Fresh bags out to the streets and given them away to the homeless people of the city. It brought tears to my eyes. I called a leader friend of mine who works at Elevation and I said, "Dude, you guys just presented one of the most powerful conferences I've ever attended. But the most powerful thing happened when I walked outside the conference and saw all those homeless people walking around with the food you'd given them. To me, that's ministry. You guys are not only reaching the people in the wealthy areas of Charlotte, the Jerusalems, Judeas, and Samarias, but you haven't forgotten the remotest places and the lowliest people."

There's a reason Elevation is the third fastest-growing church in America. I believe they've continued to keep their hearts and vision on the Bible. They have continued to reach out to those in need and to preach the gospel not only to the elite but also to the lowliest people on earth. And, like the scripture at the beginning of this chapter notes, they have received power from on high by the means of the Holy Spirit.

I was challenged big time by that incident.

If we are going to share our faith, yes, we need to witness to those God has placed in our lives—our friends and co-workers and neighbors. But if we want astounding success, let's not forget about the remotest places on earth and the lowliest people on the planet. Those who are broken and humble, those who are last and will be first. We can be the ones who help them put their very hands on the door that leads to God.

To reinforce that, let me tell you about a kid I met at Southern Wesleyan University in Central, South Carolina. After I spoke to the students on campus I was asked to teach a religion class. When I arrived in the room, I immediately noticed one student who did not fit in at all with the other religion majors. From head to toe, his body was covered with tattoos. He wore a rock star-style hat and the loose-fitting, faded clothes you'd see on a skateboarder.

I'm thinking, *Man, this guy really stands out, but I'm digging him.*

After I spoke to the class, the young man came up to me, we talked, and I just really connected with this kid. His name was Matt Beasley. I gave him my contact information and told him to keep in touch. Soon, Matt emailed me. "Man," he wrote, "I want to go to that place where you are, Christian. I want what you have. I'm starving to grow in my relationship with God. How can I grow?"

One of the things I did was turn Matt onto *Kingdom Building Ministries* (www.kbm.org) out of Denver, which is the group for which I'm an itinerant speaker. They have some extremely popular and successful summer programs designed to mentor and disciple young people.

Matt spent the summer with Kingdom Building, and when he came back, he was completely on fire for Christ. He'd made up his mind that, yes, he was going to witness to people in Jerusalem, Judea, and Samaria, but his *focal point* was going to be the remotest places of the earth—the lowliest people.

Soon thereafter, Matt phoned and told me he would be working in a soup kitchen for the homeless in downtown Greenville, South Carolina. The next thing I knew, he was sharing stories of how he'd had the opportunity to witness to homeless people on the streets and that many of those people were giving their lives to Christ.

Matt let me know later that he was reaching out to young people in the government housing and rough neighborhoods that surrounded him and was picking these kids up and taking them to church. His car got so packed that he couldn't take any more. "I don't know what I'm going to do," he said. "I'm making two, three, four trips. I don't know how I'm going to get them all to church!"

Matt began praying and out of the blue, some guy gave him a van. So he was packing the van with these lost kids and taking them all to church. Not long after that he called me and said, "Man, the van is full. I don't have any idea what I'm going to do next." That's when God provided him with a bus. Free! A gift. Not only that, but the guy who gave it to him offered to drive it. So now, Matt is filling his van and bus with up to fifty kids each week and taking them to church.

Not long ago, I received another call from Matt, and guess what? He's working with the homeless in Anderson, South Carolina, too. And guess what else? Someone donated a warehouse that they've opened to meet the needs of hungry, homeless people. What's more, a stranger walked up to Matt and gave him a check for $10,000.

I'm blown away. Or I should say, God blows me away!

While other religion majors are probably playing X-Box or intramurals, Matt is taking a full load of classes and going to the remotest places of the earth, to downtown homeless communities. He's witnessing and preaching and meeting the needs of homeless people at five and six in the morning. He's taking kids to church, delivering food to shelters, and getting clothing and blankets to homeless people on the streets. And people are pouring money into his ministry.

Matt now helps run a program called *The Lot Project* (www.thelotproject.net). "It all started as a crazy idea that we thought we were just making up in our heads, but it has slowly become a reality," says Matt. "God continues to show us that He is the one that put this vision on our hearts. As we started looking at what and who was around us in our everyday lives, we noticed that we encounter many different types of people. Some may be believers and others may not be. Some may be criminals and others may be saints. Any way you look at it, you are going to encounter those who don't know that Jesus loves them and that He wants to have a relationship with them.

"What do we do about that? *Love them.* That is the only answer. We have to love these people right where they are. This is in no way going to be easy, but it is a must. Personally, we believe that we will be held accountable for our interaction with the people we encounter in life. When I see someone who doesn't know Jesus, I want to do something about that. God has given all of us the gift of the Holy Spirit, and with the Holy Spirit we can do something about it."

Whatever you did for one of the least of these brothers of mine, you did for me.

(Matthew 25:40b)

Today, Matt and the growing team at *The Lot Project* provide help and hope to the poor, oppressed, and addicted. Through outreach partnerships, they seek to be a conduit between the needs on the street and the resources available in South Carolina. They provide free transportation to church for teens and adults; feed, clothe, and provide shelter to the homeless, poor, and oppressed; mentor teens; offer emergency shelter; and do street ministry.

Matt's life is a testimony. He's dedicated it to the lowliest people in the remotest parts of the earth. And God is blessing him. Who gives a young man a van, a bus, a warehouse, and a check for $10,000? I'll tell you who—people who are led by God. The point is, Matt is being faithful to fulfill God's wishes to share His love with the lowly—the least of these—and God is being faithful to bless his efforts.

If you gear your testimony to the remotest places, the lowliest people, God will open more doors than you ever would have dreamed possible. To me, this is the true gospel.

Religion that God our Father accepts as pure and faultless is this: to look after orphans and widows in their distress and to keep oneself from being polluted by the world.

(James 1:27)

Many times, churches are guilty of limiting themselves by reaching out only to the well-to-do people within their communities. Their marketing efforts, flyers, billboards, and radio spots are targeted to a specific audience, which is usually not the homeless. It's the people who have the financial ability to come and help them "build" what is thought of as the traditional American church.

I believe God blesses and anoints us when we seek those who are lowly, hungry, hurting, and broken. *Test me in this and see!*

Chapter 10
Questions to Dwell On

Read **Acts 1:8**. You have your first assignment. Before you answer the following questions, I want you to go and share your God-story at the lowliest place on earth. I want you to give your testimony to someone who hangs out and lives in this type of place. It may be a soup kitchen or a homeless shelter. It may be with someone hanging out at the top of the exit ramp holding a sign that reads: "Help." It may be with the outcast from your school or with a family that is one more missed house payment away from hitting the streets. It may be to the mission field of a Third World country, where people go weeks without food, and they sleep on the dirt floors of tiny huts. Take your focus off yourself and off your friends, the rich and beautiful, the athletic and popular, and go live out your faith and extend the hand of love. Pay attention to the response, then answer these questions.

1) What was the response? I would imagine the response you got was much different than the response you would get from your classmates or co-workers. I would imagine you learned why the rich young ruler walked away sad (Luke 18: 18-30), yet all the sick, poor, simple and helpless were always in the presence of Jesus with extended hands.

2) With this knowledge in your heart, what changes are you going to make in your ministry when it comes to sharing your testimony and making a difference? Some simple changes that can be made are getting together with your youth pastor or church leaders and planning an outreach program where you encounter these types of people on a monthly basis. Our church has an "Adopt a Block" program where we go out every month and cook-out and serve the local community; this is where the needs of the lowliest are met!

3) Read **Luke 16:19-31**. Remember this story and never forget the outcome while you are out sharing your testimony. Yes, go to Jerusalem, Judea, and Samaria, but never forget the people who are waiting for you in the lowliest places on earth, as well.

HERE'S THE JUICE:

There is nothing wrong with reaching the rich and upper class. Jesus died for all people. I just want you to be aware of the success you can have in sharing your testimony with those who are at the bottom rung of society. These are the weak and the poor, upon whom Jesus had great mercy when he walked the earth. Look at your church and other churches you have visited and recall the last time you saw someone who might represent the lowliest place on earth sitting on the pew next to Martha, the organ player, or her husband, Jim, the elder. That's why I have grown to appreciate the ministry of Elevation Church—they are reaching "those at the bottom." It is indeed one of the most powerful churches I've experienced in a long time. I guess I'm asking you to set your standards *low*! Go get 'em!

11 - Keeping it Real

As for you, the anointing you received from him remains in you, and you do not need anyone to teach you. But as his anointing teaches you about all things and as that anointing is real, not counterfeit— just as it has taught you, remain in him.

(1 John 2:27)

THE RESULTS FROM A RECENT POLL declared that most people who do not believe in Jesus Christ base that unbelief on the stance that the majority of self-proclaimed Christians are hypocrites. The Christian Chapman translation: when unbelievers see people who claim to be Christians, they often see a lot of counterfeit things happening in those people's lives, along with ugly two-faced behavior that discredits Christianity and gives true believers a bad name. Bottom line: the unbeliever doesn't sense that the Christian's walk and testimony is real or genuine and, therefore, wants nothing to do with the supposed Christian life.

For a testimony to be powerful and life-changing these days, it must be real. Nobody wants to build his or her life on a lie. My friend Dwight Knight, who travels, debates, and teaches apologetics across the country, including at our nation's finest Ivy League schools, once said, "People will not die for a lie." The disciples of the Bible gave their lives for something they believed was true and real—a relationship with Jesus. Dwight would affirm that those disciples would never have died for a lie. They gave their lives for something that was factual— an intimate friendship with Jesus Christ, the Great One who transformed them and gave them new life.

Does being "real" mean we're perfect? Of course not. But it does mean that each morning we wake up, we set out to live our lives in obedience to Jesus Christ, praying that, because the Holy Spirit dwells in us, our lives will bear beautiful fruit and we will lead others into a relationship with Him.

> *But the fruit of the Spirit is love, joy, peace, patience, kindness, goodness, faithfulness, gentleness and self-control. Against such things there is no law. Those who belong to Christ Jesus have crucified the sinful nature with its passions and desires. Since we live by the Spirit, let us keep in step with the Spirit.*
>
> (Galatians 5:22-25)

In other words, let our lives and our testimony be *real*.

When the Holy Spirit is real in our lives, it's obvious. We are salt, making others thirsty. We are light, guiding the way for those around us. We are living water, sweeping others up in the tide of our love.

Are you the real deal?

Are the words of your testimony backed up by a life that is pure and true?

> *For my flesh is real food and my blood is real drink.*
>
> (John 6:55)

> *These are a shadow of the things that were to come; the reality, however, is found in Christ.*
>
> (Colossians 2:17)

Get rid of the old yeast that you may be a new batch without yeast—as you really are. For Christ, our Passover lamb, has been sacrificed.

(1 Corinthians 5:7)

If you really knew me, you would know my Father as well. From now on, you do know him and have seen him.

(John 14:7)

A while back, I would find out how "true" my testimony was before an audience of millions. You see, my name was chosen out of 15,000 applicants to appear on the reality television show *Reality Racing: The Rookie Challenge*. From the moment my name was selected, I was excited (that's an understatement)!

The selection process was grueling. Out of the 15,000 applicants, a group of judges narrowed the potential participants to two hundred. For that segment of the show, I traveled to Cincinnati where I got to meet one of NASCAR's greatest champions, Bobby Allison, who was one of the judges on the program. From two hundred participants the field was narrowed to the final sixteen who would appear on the show, and by God's grace, I was one of them.

I've always been a huge race fan. My Dad used to be a professional dragster and motorcycle racer, so racing has always been in my blood. I considered the *Reality Racing* show a chance for me to really show the world what I could do. Not only would the winner earn $750,000, but he or she would also walk away with a NASCAR contract!

The only problem was, at that time in my life, although I was a huge race fan, I had very little experience actually racing. I'd driven some, but not in any serious competition, so I knew it was going to be intimidating. I would be racing against some professional drivers. In fact, a lot of guys who made the final sixteen on the show were road race and dirt race champions.

The final sixteen contestants traveled to Bronson Motor Speedway in Florida, where we participated in all kinds of races and challenges like the solo pit stop run, which tested not only our driving skills, but our physical and mental skills as well.

We were told by show officials that there would be twelve episodes of *Reality Racing: The Rookie Challenge*, each to be seen on Spike TV; so, we were talking about a huge audience. After nine episodes the field of sixteen contestants would be reduced to five, and the final three episodes would show the five finalists competing for first prize—$750,000 and the NASCAR contract.

Of course, I had dreams of a new house and me on the NASCAR circuit. You know, I was pumped! And truly, I had reason to be excited as the episodes unfolded. Why? Because after a bunch of races and eliminations, and after nine episodes of the show were taped, I was the *leader* of the whole thing with 195 points tallied! I was feeling like I could really win the thing.

Now, understand, while we were filming the shows, I tried to keep my head and just be myself. I prayed a lot about not getting over-excited about the prize and about maintaining a vibrant Christian walk above all else. I tried to keep things loose on the set and there was a lot of humor and enjoyment. We really had a great time.

During the taping, I had the pleasure of meeting an L.A. producer and the director of *Reality Racing*, Del Weston. Del is a whale of a man, standing about six-feet, seven-inches tall and probably weighing in at a good 300 pounds. He's also a former golden glove boxer and cage fighter who starred in *Rocky V* as one of the opposing boxers.

Over the course of the taping, Del and I developed a fantastic relationship. From day one, we hit it off. We talked junk and bantered back and forth. He knew I was a Christian and a pastor. As a matter of fact, he created the nickname "The Faster Pastor" for me while I was on the show.

I talked smack and was my usual self, just loving people and giving all I had in each race. Each time I had the opportunity while on camera, I talked straight-up about God. At one point, they needed someone to do a commercial for one of their sponsors and they asked me to do it instead of an actor. I was glad to help out and loved getting my feet wet in front of the camera.

During the taping for the first nine episodes, I began to sense that the show was on a tight budget. When I returned home after the nine episodes had been taped, I even began wondering if they would have enough money to finish the show. I didn't say anything about my suspicions to anyone.

Our family and friends got a kick out of watching episodes of the show on TV. And, apparently, so did a lot of other people. An average of seven million viewers watched the show each week it was on. However, after eight or nine episodes, my suspicions became reality. It was announced that, due to sponsorship problems, the show would stop airing and the last three episodes would not be filmed.

So much for the $750,000 and the NASCAR contract.

"Christian, you were in the lead!" my wife said. "We're talking about $750,000. You need to follow up on this and see what's going on." Believe me, I understood Amy's frustration. But we both took a deep breath.

"No," I said. "I know God had me on there for a purpose. We'll find out what that purpose is, but I'm cool with it as it is. We'll just let God work it out."

As it turned out, Del Weston phoned me personally to apologize about the show being canceled. He knew I was excited, especially because I was leading as we headed into the final five showdown.

"Man, don't worry about it," I said. "God uses all things for His glory."

There was a long pause. "Christian," he said, "I want you to know you've really impacted my life. In fact, I'd like to fly you out here to L.A. I'll take care of you while you're out here. I'd like you to dedicate my little girl to the Lord, out here in the ocean, in Orange County. Would you do that?"

Would I? Yes! And what an awesome experience it was. Standing on that beach. Holding that little girl in my arms. Anointing her head with oil. Praying over her. Asking God to watch over her life, to work in her life. And looking at this big six-foot, seven-inch, 300 pound man, just weeping like a child.

Living in that really cool and incomparable moment among new friends and honoring God as we were, I realized that *that* was the real prize in the whole episode. To see Del and his family drawing close to God. That was worth more than anything I could put a price tag on, and certainly worth much more than $750,000 and a NASCAR contract. Would I have loved to have had those things? Absolutely. But the most important thing to me is that I make an impact for God. I think I did that by being real.

When I talked to Del and got to know him, I think what turned him on to the gospel of Jesus was the fact that I was just a real guy who acknowledged his sinfulness and openly gave praise to God for saving me. "I've never met anyone like you," Del once said.

During one of the takes we were doing for the show, Del yelled "Cut" and we had a short break before going back to another action scene. That's when he approached me. "Man," he said. "I want you to take some time to explain to me why you are like a breath of fresh air when you walk onto this set. I sense it. Other people sense it. I want you to talk to me about that."

I had many conversations with Del about the life I lived and what made it special, namely, my relationship with Jesus Christ. I got to testify. He looked at my life and he realized I was a real person and that there was nothing counterfeit. Because of that, he made a change in his life that would ultimately change his entire family. As a matter of fact, he told me not long ago that he wanted to get into making family films and positive projects that will make a difference in the world. I have all the confidence that he will do just that.

"In television we see people from every stripe," Del said. "When you add the desperation and possibilities of wealth and fame that accompany reality television, all bets are off. That being said, Christian Chapman brought an air of class, charm, and integrity to the *Reality Racing* set. He never flaunted his religion, but he didn't shy away from his spirituality or compromise it at any time, either.

"On the days that I had the pleasure of working with him, his faith was front and center during some grueling challenges and under tremendous pressure. If it is true that having money reveals who you are, then winning his episode and cash to-boot only proved Chapman to be a man of God. What many people don't know is that even though the show was stopped near the end of the season, the first ten episodes were shot and in the can. Of all the contestants who appeared on the show, only one had what it truly took to be called a champion of *Reality Racing: The Rookie Challenge*, and that was Christian Chapman. Not to take anything away from any of the other contestants, because many of them were fantastic and had the skills behind the wheel. But when you take everything into account—points, driving, talent, personality, charisma, and integrity—Christian would have been crowned the champion. Period."

One of the most eye-opening events in the whole saga happened months after the show got canceled. That's when Del told me that many of the contestants had called to complain, bashed the show on the Internet, and even threatened to bring lawsuits when they heard the show had been canceled. He said that when he saw the firestorm that was going down and found out that my name was not a part of all the negative fallout, that's when he knew that my life was the "real deal." Del realized that the Christ I had proclaimed while living and working with him on the show was not counterfeit but real, dependable, and trustworthy.

If we are going to dare to testify, we had better make sure that what goes on in our lives is not counterfeit.

> *Some Jews who went around driving out evil spirits tried to invoke the name of the Lord Jesus over those who were demon-possessed. They would say, "In the name of Jesus, whom Paul preaches, I command you to come out." Seven sons of Sceva, a Jewish chief priest, were doing this. (One day) the evil spirit an swered them, "Jesus I know, and I know about Paul, but who are you?" Then the man who had the evil spirit jumped on them and overpowered them all. He gave them such a beating that they ran*

out of the house naked and bleeding.

(Acts 19:13-16)

To me, that is one of the funniest stories in the Bible.

Why?

Here these guys were, trying to cast out this demon just by mentioning the name of Jesus. Were they even believers? Did they have true faith? Were their lives a genuine testimony or were they counterfeits? Was their faith real or not? One thing we know for sure is that the guy to whom they were trying to cast out the demon did not associate them with Jesus or Paul. He said, "Jesus I know, and I know about Paul, but who are you dudes?" Then the evil spirit in that man pounced on those guys and he gave them a beat down they would never forget.

Even the devil recognized that those guys were counterfeits.

What about you? Are you the real deal?

Eighty-seven percent of Americans claim they are Protestant Christians. But living in this country, we know full well that's not true. We have scores of counterfeit products out there and now more than ever we need Christians to be real. We need our testimonies to be solid as a rock and the layers of our character to be clean and transparent. We need to be a breath of fresh air in a world that is gasping on the poisonous gases of sin, lies, materialism, selfishness, and deceit.

What does all of this mean to you on a personal level? If there is habitual sin in your life, cry out to God in repentance. Get your conscience clear before Jesus. Otherwise, all of your "good works" are going to be burned up like chaff. Dive into the word of God daily. Know that you know that you know that you have a strong, unbreakable relationship with the Son of God. Pray and worship Him in Spirit and truth. And lean on the Holy Spirit to bear much good fruit through your life.

In closing, my eight-year-old son Malachi did his first oral book report at school the other day. He dressed up like Abraham Lincoln and read some of Lincoln's famous words. Malachi had to learn a lot about Lincoln's childhood and, at one point, he came up to me and said, "Dad, did you know Abraham Lincoln couldn't read or write when he was young, and neither could his mother? But he knew God's Word!"

"He did?" I said. "How could he know God's Word if he couldn't read or write, and if his mother couldn't?" Malachi went on to explain to me that Lincoln's mother had memorized tons of scripture simply by listening intently to sermons and to other people read the Bible aloud. Every night, she would rehash the scripture in her mind, internalize it, feed on it, and recite it. Her practice of doing so had a lot to do with Abraham Lincoln making a stand against slavery in the south. He was grounded in the Word of God. As a result, slavery was abolished.

Well, since the *Reality Racing* show, I've gained a great deal more experience racing and will even participate in the Baja 1000 this year, doing 100 mph in the middle of the desert. I love it. And what I love equally as much is getting to minister at a children's orphanage while we're doing the race, and speaking in San Felipe, and giving out Bibles in Mexico.

You see, what I am learning is that there is much more to life than just "talking" a good game. Each day of our lives we have a chance to worship God in the things we say and do. And what does the Bible tell us? It says to worship Him in "spirit and in truth."

> *No one lights a lamp and puts it in a place where it will be hidden, or under a bowl. Instead he puts it on its stand, so that those who come in may see the light. Your eye is the lamp of your body. When your eyes are good, your whole body also is full of light. But when they are bad, your body also is full of darkness. See to it, then, that the light within you is not darkness. Therefore, if your whole body is full of light, and no part of it dark, it will be completely lighted, as when the light of a lamp shines on you."*
>
> (Luke 11: 33-36)

Chapter 11
Questions to Dwell On

We live in a world where there is a test for everything. That being said, allow me to jump on the bandwagon and do something a little different in this chapter. I am going to give you a five-question test to help you determine whether or not you're the "real deal." Be honest now...

1) Does your relationship with Jesus come before any other relationship you have? (See Matthew 6:33; Matthew 22:37-40.)

2) Do you find yourself enjoying this life and what this world has to offer more than the thought of being with Jesus? (See Philippians 1:21; Matthew 10:39.) Fill in the blank for the following: "No one can serve two masters. Either he will hate the one and love the other, or he will be devoted to the one and despise the other, you cannot serve both God and __________." (See Matthew 6:24.)

3) Do you let the world dictate how you walk out your faith? Examples: your job, your school, your friends, and yes, even your church. (See Galatians 2:11-14; Acts 4:20.)

4) Do you find yourself dwelling on how you can improve *your* situation or that of someone less fortunate? In other words, do you desire getting served more than you do serving others? (See Luke 10:38-42; Ephesians 6:7; 1 Peter 4:10.)

5) Do people recognize you as a radical follower of Jesus Christ, or someone who is just walking through life? (See Matthew 12:33; Luke 6:44.)

HERE'S THE JUICE:

Recently I did a camp where a young lady re-committed her life to Jesus and started radically sharing her faith with her friends. She emailed me several weeks later and said one of her best friends gave her life to Christ after she witnessed to her. The friend said she never knew this girl was a Christian and that she had not known that living with Jesus was so important to her. When her friend experienced this girl's passion, the friend wanted it as well and her life was changed forever. People need to recognize you as the real deal. That's exactly what made a difference in the life of one Hollywood director, and it will make a difference in the lives you encounter as well. So keep it real!

12 - Risk it All

Then he called the crowd to him along with his disciples and said: "If anyone would come after me, he must deny himself and take up his cross and follow me. For whoever wants to save his life will lose it, but whoever loses his life for me and for the gospel will save it. What good is it for a man to gain the whole world, yet forfeit his soul? Or what can a man give in exchange for his soul? If anyone is ashamed of me and my words in this adulterous and sinful generation, the Son of Man will be ashamed of him when he comes in his Father's glory with the holy angels.

(Mark 8:34-38)

BEFORE JESUS CHRIST LEFT THE EARTH, he told his disciple Peter to get ready because a day would come when Peter would have to meet the same death Jesus was going to meet. History tells us Peter was indeed crucified, but when it was time for him to be nailed to the cross, he claimed that he had no right to die the same way his Lord and Savior had, so Peter was crucified upside down.

> *I tell you the truth, when you were younger you dressed yourself and went where you wanted; but when you are old you will stretch out your hands, and someone else will dress you and lead you where you do not want to go." Jesus said this to indicate the kind of death by which Peter would glorify God. Then he said to him, "Follow me!"*
>
> (John 21:18, 19)

This is the point in Peter's life when Jesus said to him, "Feed My sheep." Jesus knew it wasn't going to be easy for Peter after He was gone. He was basically telling Peter, "Even though I know it is going to cost you your life, I am asking you to testify. Peter, you are going to need to *risk it all*!" After Jesus was crucified, Peter never backed down. He had risk it all.

> *Then they called them in again and commanded them not to speak or teach at all in the name of Jesus. But Peter and John replied, "Judge for yourselves whether it is right in God's sight to obey you rather than God. For we cannot help speaking about what we have seen and heard."*
>
> (Acts 4:18-20)

At times in life we might risk a friendship, a job, or a relationship. We might take risks on the athletic field or in the stock market. But to me, there is nothing more serious or meaningful or powerful than being ready to lay down our lives for God and for others so someone else can believe in Jesus Christ and have eternal life.

Back when I was a youth pastor in Charleston, South Carolina, there was a group of young men with whom I fell in love. We were close. We were connected. When we got together, the fellowship and brotherhood just overflowed. One time, we decided we were going to venture out to Hickory Knob State Park to camp, eat, hang out, and fellowship.

I gathered these kids up, we packed it in and took off for this beautiful park. As soon as we arrived at our campsite, the guys ganged up on me and told me they wanted to go into town and get something to eat.

"We just got here!" I said. "Don't be wimps! This is nature, man, this is what we came for, and you already want to go to town, back to civilization?"

"Come on Christian, we want to get some fast-food burgers and cruise the town!"

I gave in. We all piled in the car and I began driving around, trying to find "town." Soon we found ourselves on this ancient road that looked like it had existed for centuries. Off to the right we saw this sign for some historical site, some seven miles down this long dirt road, deep into the woods. There was barely room for one car on this dirt road. The sun was setting. And the trees had grown over the road, joining together so it looked like you were driving into a dark tunnel.

"There! Let's take that road," they yelled. "Let's see what's down there!" They were going crazy. "It's a historical site. We can tell our moms and dads we learned something educational!"

"Dude, we are not going down that road," I said. "Let's stick to the plan and go find this town. I'm starving."

"Come on Christian, you didn't even want to go get anything to eat when we left. Forget the food. Let's go see what's down that dirt road!" I mean, they were losing it.

"No. I'm overriding that junk. This is my wife's car. I'm not taking it down that old dirt road. We're going this way. We're gonna grab some food and go back to the campsite."

They screamed, yelled, and complained, but we went to town, found a Burger King, got something to eat, and headed back toward the campsite.

Now it was dark.

And again, we came to the dirt road.

They went berserk. "Go for it! Let's do the dirt road! We gotta see what's down there." Then the name-calling began. "You're yellow! Come on, you coward! Chicken! I double-dog dare you! I triple-dog dare you!"

The manly talk got real deep.

"Alright," I gave in. "You wanna see what's down there? Let's go."

So we begin down this dark, dirt sliver of road in my wife's brand new Honda. About a mile and a half into the middle of nowhere, we came to an intersection with an old, dilapidated farmhouse tucked off to the side of the road. In one of the windows, a sole candle burned. It was so stinking creepy, I can't even begin to tell you. Cold chills enveloped me.

Beyond the house, barely visible in the dark, was a big barn. Its doors were wide open. Farm tools like cycles and pitchforks swung back and forth in the breeze. It looked like the *Texas Chainsaw Massacre* house. My Dad messed up and let me watch that movie when I was about twelve and I've *never* forgotten it.

"We need to turn around and roll on outta here," I said.

The name-calling began again. "We're committed! Come on, there's no turning back now! Let's go check it out!" I mean, these guys were ruthless.

So we kept driving. And soon we came to an old bridge. A sign on it read: "Built by Army engineers in 1908. Proceed with caution."

"Come on!" they yelled. "Let's go see."

I'm thinking my wife's Honda is going to plunge to its watery grave, but we continued on. The bridge creaked. Boards literally cracked as we crept over it. The guys are yelling and carrying on.

I was terrified, but we kept going. We must have been five or six miles into the woods when I turned to the group and said, "Guys, there is nothing back here. We are heading to the campsite."

Just then, one of the guys yells, "Dude! Straight ahead!

I flipped my lights to high beam only to reveal a huge tombstone. We must have each made out the words on the stone at the same time: *Indian Massacre Site.*

I drove forward, turned slightly, and we all read the story on the stone. As it turns out, some 140 men, women, and children were brutally massacred at this site by wild, renegade Indians. The people had been traveling across several states on their way to receive free land and to get a new start on life.

Surely, those people knew the danger of taking their women and children across the barren country in those days. They knew the risk, they took it, and they paid the ultimate price. But they went because it was something they had to do. Back in those days, to be butchered by an Indian was no quick death. They had been brutally murdered, probably with knives and arrows, and likely scalped.

"Nobody get out of this car," I instructed. "We are turning around and we are leaving right now."

"Let's go see where they're buried!" one of them yelled. He had read the small print at the bottom of the tombstone, which said that some one hundred yards further down the road was a large burial mound where all of those poor people were buried.

Against my better judgment, we got out of the car and began to walk down this ancient path. The wind was blowing. Branches were whipping and cracking in the wind. I could have sworn I heard Indian drums. Then we came upon it—a huge mound where those 140 people had been laid to rest.

Everyone fell dead silent. Not a word.

BAM! It hit me.

"Christian," I thought. "You have the *only* keys to the *only* car, seven miles deep in a haunted forest. For the last thirty minutes these boys have ridiculed you and repeatedly called you a yellow coward chicken. Now, what are you going to do about it?"

I took off running to the car, still formulating the plan in my head to lock the doors when I get in and leave them out there in the haunted forest with the burial mound. Then we would see what they were all about.

"Oh, no!" one of the boys screamed. "Don't leave Christian!"

They came after me like a pack of wolf hounds.

I dove into the driver's seat and locked all the doors. Soon I had teenagers jumping on the hood, hoisting themselves onto the roof, pounding on the trunk. One or two were almost in tears. I had the windshield wipers going as I was spraying them with wiper fluid. And there we went, bumping out of the woods at about 30 mph with these kids hanging off my car.

Then I began hearing the bells of the cash registers of insurance companies in my head and determined it would be very wise of the youth pastor to pull over, so I did. I tell people all the time that God definitely has His hands on youth ministry all across our country, because youth pastors do some crazy things. Driving with kids on the car was something I should not have done, but man, did I laugh. I think I heard one of them call out for his mother.

Finally, I let them all back in the car and no one said a word but me. I was laughing. Each of them was pale as a ghost. We drove out of the woods. I was making fun of them. Then, all of the sudden, I heard God speak to me. *Christian,* He said, *140 people lost their lives to get a free piece of land, and I can't get you to risk your life for anything. You have a nice, cushy job. You don't share your faith. You never get outside your comfortable little box.*

This was early on in my ministry, and His voice was true. I had a nice paying job at a great church with a fantastic youth group, a big Christmas bonus, and my own children got to attend the Christian school for free. I had everything I could have ever needed or wanted in life, but I wasn't sharing my faith radically. I wasn't living outside the box. I wasn't taking any risks for God. And I really didn't feel like I was making a big difference for the kingdom.

Looking back, the Indian massacre site served as a turning point in my life and ministry. That was when I began stepping out more boldly and sharing what God had done in my life. And as I saw results, a little at a time, my confidence grew. Soon, I was sharing my testimony whenever, wherever, and with whomever I could.

We need to take risks, to live outside the box. Take a walk on the wild side for the kingdom of God. This is not our home down here. Our home is in heaven. We have eternity to bask in glory. But down here during this brief time we have on earth, let us be about His business—and let us be radical about it.

Remember, Jesus told Peter, "Get out of the boat. I don't want you to stay where it's comfortable. I want you to do the impossible. Walk on water. Come out where the storm is, because it is in that moment that it won't be about you, it will be about what I can do *through* you."

My challenge to you is to begin to share God in such a way as you never would have dreamed of before. When you do that, you won't be able to do it in the flesh, you'll be forced to depend on the Holy Spirit. It's going to be all Him, which is exactly what He wants.

After Peter had denied Jesus three times, after the crucifixion, Jesus called Peter to come in from his boat. Jesus was waiting for him with some fresh fish on the fire. "Do you love Me?" he asked.

"You know I do, Lord."

"Feed my sheep."

In other words, *testify*!

Go out and share your faith. Do what I've called you to do. It may cost you your life. But that is a risk you'll have to take.

A friend of mine, Clayton King, told a story one time that I've never forgotten. Here's a guy who has done some radical things in his life. I think he started preaching when he was about fourteen, and he's continued to do so for the past twenty years. He's an amazing speaker.

Well, God called Clayton to go to the Himalayas, to a remote village where no other missionary had ever taken Bibles or medical supplies. Even after he drove two days, it was going to require an additional fifty-mile hike through the mountains to make it to this small village.

When he met up with his guides, they told Clayton that four European missionaries had just had their heads cut off for bringing eleven Bibles out and attempting to share their faith. Clayton had 1,100 Bibles! He was terrified. Along the way he encountered a dude wearing camouflage fatigues and carrying an M-16. "You can go no further," the soldier said.

"Dude, we need to get to this place," Clayton said. "You need to let us go."

"No. You see the smoke over the mountain?"

Clayton looked and saw.

"They just bombed one of the villages," the soldier said. "They're carrying dead bodies out now. I can't let you go."

"I'm going to pay you some money, and you let me go," Clayton handed him one hundred rupees and the man let him go. Soon they were rambling down the road and the driver insisted they pick up a hitchhiker who was wearing a Members Only jacket and some glasses that looked like Elvis's.

"I'm a king," the hitchhiker said when he got in the car.

"King of what?" Clayton asked.

"I'm the king of the village you are headed to. I'm leaving to go speak at another village. My car broke down. I need a ride. What is your name?"

"Clayton King."

"Oh, you are a king, too?"

In that part of the world your last name is indicative of what you are.

"If you are going to my village, let me give you a note, signed from me. This will give you clearance to get into my village with your Bibles. Show this to anyone who causes you trouble, and you will be well. You can serve as the king of my village while I am away."

I laugh about this now, but it is a true story. At the same time, I have tears in my eyes because I think of what a powerful work of God that was. You talk about God showing up? Clayton made it to the village. He gave out tons of Bibles and medical supplies, and he actually got to live as the king because he had a hand-written note from the real king.

There was somewhat of an uproar, and the people came to him. "Come," they said. "A woman is about to give birth. We need your help." Several medical volunteers had traveled with Clayton, so they went and found the pregnant woman. They found her lying on a dirt floor on a burlap sack with blood all around her. For thirty hours, she had been in heavy labor.

The medical volunteer knelt down, examined her, and turned to Clayton, "You need to pray right now. This woman has twins in there and one of them is locked in sideways. He may die."

At that instant, Clayton realized that if one of the babies came out dead, and he was this new king that had wandered in to rule, the people of the village would probably kill him. He'd been going on and on about Jesus and His miracles. He'd been handing out Bibles. If his talk and his God weren't real, he was likely dead meat.

Clayton stood. He found a translator. And he declared to that village, "These babies are going to live!" He felt that if God could part the Red Sea but would not save those babies, then what he and his team had been saying would be viewed as a lie and those villagers would have had every right to kill every last one of his team.

Clayton's medical volunteer turned to him and said, "Clayton, I hope you are telling the truth. I hope God told you to say that, because I'm looking at one of the babies now, and I know it's dead." She'd had to break one of the baby's legs to get it out.

Indeed, the one baby was dead when they got it out. It had been dead for some time, possibly hours. Its flesh was cold. The other baby came out alive and well. Clayton immediately started praying over the dead infant.

Jesus Christ resurrected that baby on the spot.

That baby came back to life!

Clayton soon realized that this whole journey had begun a long time ago when he had decided to take a risk and go to the Himalayas as God had prompted him to do. Four Europeans had been decapitated just prior to his arrival. The place was being bombed. Dead body parts were being carted out in droves. He encountered the king, who found favor on him. Then came the test of the pregnant woman in labor with the twins.

Through it all, Clayton moved forward. Why? Because God had called him to step out and take the risk. If Clayton died, so be it. At least he would have gone down doing what he was supposed to be doing.

The same could be said of four desperate lepers whose story is told in the Old Testament. Look at their desperation. Examine their faith. See how they stepped outside the box. And watch how they testified.

Now there were four men with leprosy at the entrance of the city gate. They said to each other, "Why stay here until we die? If we say, 'We'll go into the city' - the famine is there, and we will die. And if we stay here, we will die. So let's go over to the camp of the Arameans and surrender. If they spare us, we live; if they kill us, then we die."

(2 Kings 7:3, 4)

Stay with me now, reader, and understand that this famine these guys are facing is deathly. In fact, a chapter earlier, two women actually boiled one of their babies to eat. These four lepers are about to die. The Arameans are their devout enemies. Yet, they are considering going into their camp. Let's read on:

At dusk they got up and went to the camp of the Arameans. When they reached the edge of the camp, not a man was there, for the Lord had caused the Arameans to hear the sound of chariots and horses and a great army, so that they said to one another, "Look, the king of Israel has hired the Hittite and Egyp tian kings to attack us!" So they got up and fled in the dusk and abandoned their tents and their horses and donkeys. They left the camp as it was and ran for their lives.

(2 Kings 7:5-7)

Do you see what happens when we get desperate and step out in faith? God moves mountains as well as enemies. Here, he caused the Aramean army to think they heard the sound of chariots and horses, so they ran in fear. When the lepers arrived, they found an empty city full of food, clothing, and anything they needed. But the account doesn't end there.

The men who had leprosy reached the edge of the camp and entered one of the tents. They ate and drank, and carried away silver, gold and clothes, and went off and hid them. They returned and entered another tent and took some things from it and hid them also. Then they said to each other, "We're not doing right. This is a day of good news and we are keeping it to ourselves. If we wait until daylight, punishment will overtake us. Let's go at once and report this to the royal palace."

(2 Kings 7: 8, 9)

At first, the lepers simply ate, drank, and got their fill. They wallowed in the treasures they had found. But then their consciences began to bother them and they realized that, after the miracle that had happened to them, they had to go and share their story.

It is the exact same with us. We are living, walking, talking, breathing miracles. Our lives have been transformed by a King who took insults, whips, and a cross of crucifixion for us so that we could die to sin and live for Him. If indeed we are living for Him, isn't it time we got out of our comfort zones and started sharing our stories?

What's happened to you—your faith in God—is *GOOD* news. It is news that can literally alter the lives and eternities of other desperate people. Do you have the faith and courage to share it? Even in the enemy camp? School? Your workplace? The story of the lepers clearly shows that God blesses us when we move out in faith and desperation.

The longer I go on in life and in faith, the more I realize that risks can pay enormous dividends. God loves it when we risk it all for Him.

That's what this book is about.

That's what your life is about.

And now it's your turn.

Testify!

Chapter 12
Questions to Dwell On

Read **Mark 8: 34-38**. We are winding things down, but not before the most important of all chapters. As I'm sure you learned from the story of the pioneers, risking it all calls us to lay it all on the line. But before I suggest you make such a costly decision, read these questions and make sure you are truly ready.

1) Do you truly know our sovereign God and have a personal love relationship with His Son Jesus? (See John 21:15-19; Galatians 2:20.)

2) Are you ready to fulfill the call God has on your life, even if it costs you everything? (See Acts 20:22-24.)

3) If you were to lay your life on the line for God, would you have any regrets about the life you would leave behind? Would you feel like you would be missing out on unfulfilled goals you'd hoped to achieve later in life? Remember the story of Rich, the man who died in my arms from a sudden heart attack? Sometimes we don't have tomorrow to live out our dreams and desires.

Read the story of Stephen, the first martyr of the New Testament church, in Acts 6:8–7:60. In this story we see that Stephen had only enough time for one sermon after he received the call to risk it all, but God used him in a radical way to build the foundation for the early church. Stephen's answers to the above questions would have been yes, yes, and no. If yours are the same, then you are ready. If they're not, then I want you to connect with one of the pastors at your church and find out why. We need Christians today who are ready to risk it all to see the kingdom of God advance in a way that it did in the book of Acts. So, are you ready to *risk it all*?

HERE'S THE JUICE:

One of my favorite cowboy movies is *Unforgiven* with Clint Eastwood. Near the end of the film when the enemy posse is about to ride into town for the final shootout, one of the young gunslingers is talking about death and facing the end. Clint Eastwood looks at the young kid with his famous squint and, in a stern voice says, "It's a heck of a thing to kill a man. You take all he's got, and all he's ever gonna have." Not true for the Christian, but as it applies to earthly terms, right on the money. The interesting thing is that after this statement the kid backs out, but cool Clint still rides into town and takes care of business. That's the way this book will work with some. After reading it some will start to live out your faith in a radical way, looking for opportunities around every corner to testify and watch God work. Others will simply lay it down and step away as if it was the wrong call for the wrong person. My call and faith walk is my responsibility, and yours is not my business, but I pray that this book and especially this chapter will cause you to reflect on the effectiveness of your life in a lost and dying world.

13 - Finish Strong

However, I consider my life worth nothing to me,
if only I may finish the race
and complete the task the Lord Jesus has given me—
the task of testifying to the gospel of God's grace.

(Acts 20: 24)

THINK ABOUT WHAT PAUL WAS SAYING; basically: "My life is worth *nothing* unless I am testifying." Remember when he said, "To live is Christ, to die is gain." What does that mean? It means that when he was living, Paul himself was a living sacrifice. His life was about God. Why? The Lord had transformed him and he, in turn, had determined to live his life with the candle burning at both ends, full out, pedal to the metal, spreading the good news about Jesus Christ. And when he died, it would be even better because he would be with his Savior, forever.

Oh, to live like that today.

But we have so many people who call themselves Christians that go to church on Sunday, who go to work, interact with friends and family, venture out to eat, go to the mall and around town, go to movies, socialize with an array of people, yet they *never* mention the name of Jesus.

They may lift their hands in church, read their Bibles throughout the week, sing worship songs (even lead worship), hear the challenges of their pastors, but they walk out of church and leave everything at the door.

A friend recently told me he believes the problem with today's church is that we have replaced the "go and tell" with the "come and see." The job of the church is to equip believers so we can be better armed to go out and share the gospel and our testimonies.

Were you aware that when Jesus gave the Great Commission—commanding us to be His witnesses in Jerusalem, Judea, Samaria, and to the ends of the earth—that the term "Great Commission" literally means to "tell as we go." Our lives should be living, breathing instruments and vessels through which God's Spirit is actively and vibrantly testifying.

Paul implied that he considered his life worth *nothing* unless he finished the race, and that race involved testifying about the gospel of Jesus Christ. In fact, I don't think Paul even felt he was running the race unless he was testifying. What good is life and all the material possessions if there is no meaning?

> *What good is it for a man to gain the whole world, yet forfeit his soul?*
>
> (Mark 8:36)

Let's not deceive ourselves. Can we humble ourselves for a minute and be open to some reproof? How can we call ourselves Christians (which literally means "Christ-follower") if we don't even mumble the name of our Lord? Would He have wanted us to get saved, figure our eternity in heaven was secured, then go back to living like the world?

No. In fact He would cry out against such self-centeredness.

Do not conform any longer to the pattern of this world, but be transformed by the renewing of your mind.

(Romans 12:2a)

It's my personal belief that we cannot truly call ourselves Christians if we are not actively sharing our faith. Paul would say, "How can you even say you're running the race if you are not testifying about the gospel of Jesus Christ? It is why we live and breath and have our being!"

I want to share one last story with you that I hope will solidify in your mind the dire importance of a testimony and the eternal consequences your testimony can have in the lives of others (starting today).

One day I received a call from a woman named Tina, with whom I had gone to high school. Tina had heard I was a chaplain for NASCAR and MRO Racing, and she let me know that NASCAR was coming to Charlotte Motor Speedway, and that her eighteen-year-old son was going to be racing in one of the smaller events leading up to big race.

For the first time in Tina's son's life, he would be driving at speeds up to 150 miles per hour, before a crowd of some 150,000 spectators. She was terrified.

"Christian," she said, "could you come up here and pray for my son before he races? I know it's a lot to ask."

I said yes, drove to Charlotte, found her and her son, and prayed with them. Next, the kid took to the track and I was situated in the pits with his mom, family, and friends. After ten or fifteen laps, all of the cars were bunched up. They came out of turn four and a car that looked like Tina's son's began to spin out.

She screamed. The car spun down to the infield, onto the grass, then hit an interior asphalt track, which launched the vehicle into the air. The car flipped seven or eight times right in front of us. It was like slow motion, with pieces of the car flying off everywhere. Sheet metal was falling off. Gas and flames shot out. It looked like a bomb had gone off.

When the car banged to a smoky stop it somehow landed on all four tires, but the tires were about all that was left. There wasn't an ounce of metal left, only the metal bars that formed the roll cage and the cockpit where the driver sits. I could see the driver's body and he was not moving. At that instant, Tina must have thought her boy was dead.

The crowd was silent.

Then we noticed the driver's head move slightly.

"That isn't him! It isn't him!" Tina cried. And she was right, the driver turned out not to be her boy.

Reaching down, the driver unbuckled his safety belt. Slowly, he stood up through the roll cage and extended his hand into the air. Then he began to pump his arms in the air and nod, as if he was yelling in celebration. The crowd broke into a celebratory scream that could probably be heard four counties over.

I got chills. Why? For the same reason the crowd was going berserk. Not because this guy was an excellent driver or because he had won the race. In fact, his car was a pile of junk. No, I believe the crowd was so ecstatic because the driver himself was ecstatic. Race fans get passionate when they see drivers lay it all on the line. They love it when those cars bump and bang. Likewise, people love it when they see a genuine, transparent Christian whose life is real, whose fruit is obvious, and whose love is genuine.

Those race fans cheered because they realized the driver was passionate about what he was doing. It excited them. Sharing our testimonies will move other people and get them excited about drawing close to God and even sharing their faith.

As you contemplate what you've read in this book, as you seek God and go out to share your faith, be aware that Satan will attempt to steal, kill, and destroy what you've learned, and the zeal you now have to impact lives for Jesus.

There will even be times when you share your faith and you spin out and lose control, and maybe even flip your car, so to speak, feeling like you finished last. But know this: there are going to be 150,000 angels in heaven, just like those race fans, who are cheering you on. Even if you think you may be failing when you share your faith, know this: People in heaven are yelling and screaming because you had the true, gritty faith that propelled you to get crazy and share Jesus Christ.

As you turn the last page of this book, please know that I love you. You are why I wrote this book. I have prayed for you and every individual who will read it—that the words here will not only challenge you, but inspire you.

Now, get out there and run the race, my friend. And remember, the most important thing about the race is your testimony about the One who set you free and gave you eternal life. May your testimony shine, bubble up, spill over, flood the land, and win many souls for our King.

Peace.

Final Thoughts

I AM TRULY BLESSED that you decided to make *Testify* a part of your Christian walk. In the grand scheme of things, how much can a simple redneck like myself impact the world? I'm hoping about as much as a bunch of fishermen two thousand-plus years ago. The same goes for you. No matter where you're from, or how powerful your life has been to this point, I want you to know that you *can* make a difference. I look forward to hearing of the successes this book may help spark in your life After all, nothing is more powerful than your God-story. Just as 100,000 race fans cheered for the driver of a wrecked race car, all of heaven is ready to rejoice at your new walk with Christ. So get out there and lay it all on the line. And daily pray for new and exciting opportunities to testify and share your faith. May He bless you in many ways as you step out in a lost world with compass in hand, ready to lead them to the throne of God. I love you and pray for you daily.

Peace,
Christian Chapman